Great Western Wagons Appendix

Great Western Wagons Appendix

by J.H.Russell

Oxford Publishing Co.   Oxford

SBN 0 902888 03 X

Printed by Blackwell's in the City of Oxford.

Photo Reproduction by Oxford Litho Plates Ltd, Oxford.

The publishers wish to point out that several of the line
illustrations are taken from official drawings and due to the
age of these, the reproduction is not as clear as they would
wish.

Published by Oxford Publishing Co., 5 Lewis Close,
Risinghurst, Headington, Oxford.

'TO THE MEMORY OF MY FATHER, WHO INSTILLED IN ME
RESPECT AND REGARD FOR THE GREAT WESTERN RAILWAY.'

PHOTOGRAPHS CREDITS

Acknowledgments to British Railways Western Region for all photographs,
except those in Figs—41, 45—50, 63, 67, 70, 76, 77, 90—100, 119, 120,
123—129, 134—141, 152, 193, 194, 212—214, 246—250, 257—259, 263, 264,
272, 277, 283, 284, 293, 294, 300, 301 and 335—338 which were taken by
M. Longridge and Author.

PREFACE

Only the kind permission of the Public Relations Office at Paddington in granting access to the Photographic Sections of the Western Region has made this collection of pictures possible and worthwhile.

The old Great Western Railway Company was very record-conscious, and it would seem that any departure from the normal was duly photographed and documented, which has resulted in a massive library of pictures, not only of engines, coaches, and wagons, but of a multitude of subjects, ranging from station lavatories to portraits of Viscount Churchill.

The two departments responsible for photographs were the Civil Engineers at Paddington and the Mechanical Engineers at Swindon, both having their own cameras, darkrooms, files, and records, plus of course, expert operators.

When it became known that these files were to be dispersed and packed away in mid-1973, it was thought that a thorough search amongst the negatives, looking for objects of interest to enthusiasts, was not only vital but of great importance for posterity.

So it was that my publisher and I spent several exhausting days in the Aladdin's cave at Paddington, amongst the dust and cobwebs of 50 years, painstakingly taking down, looking at, and restoring, hundreds of large, heavy 12 in. X 10 in. glass negatives!

This small room situated way up on the roof of Paddington station, is seldom visited nowadays, and no register exists of the thousands of negatives stored there. Nevertheless, it was a privilege and a thrill to be allowed to look through this fantastic collection, and literally see the history of the Great Western Railway pass before one's eyes.

The most difficult task was to choose which negatives to ask for printing, and which to pass up. It is very necessary to be strong-minded and ruthless, otherwise it is so easy to overwhelm the dwindling resources in the photographic sections. At both Paddington and Swindon there is still a great sense of 'pride in the job', and every picture just has to be right; I would like to pay tribute to both my friends Cyril at Swindon and 'Mac' at Paddington, for their endless patience and help in the production of the official pictures.

This, then, is the background behind so many of these wagon pictures. First taken with a huge camera, some more than 50 years ago, the negatives retouched, and in some cases blocked out and finally stored, perhaps only to see the light of day again when two eager collectors, covered in dust, tired, hot, but happy, discovered them again and caused them to be published in this series, for everyone's interest and pleasure.

I only hope you find these wagon pictures as interesting to look at as I did to collect and document.

INTRODUCTION

After the success of the *Great Western Wagons* book, many readers have written asking for more! This is not only very satisfying, but also complimentary to the point of convincing me that there is still a large following of Great Western enthusiasts, even twenty-five years after the Company has ceased to exist!

Both my publisher and I were surprised at the popularity of the first wagon book, as it was primarily just a modest venture, and as such has many errors, faults, and omissions; so much so, that I have asked the publisher to print a list of those mistakes so that the record can be put reasonably straight. This list is available from the publishers on request.

I have received letters from readers throughout the world, with queries about Great Western freight stock in general, and about photographs in particular, so to try and meet this demand in some small way, and before all the material is either scrapped or dispersed, I have made many visits to both Paddington and Swindon archives, and have managed to collect quite a remarkable selection of wagon photographs. It is with these superb pictures as a nucleus that the 'Appendix' to the original wagon book is made up.

There are few drawings in this edition, being more of an album of illustrations, for the reason that access to official diagrams is now extremely difficult. In fact, many just do not exist, which is hardly surprising when one considers that some of the vehicles depicted have been withdrawn for upwards of 50 years! But my publisher hopes to publish a further volume of just wagon drawings at a later date.

I have taken advantage of this second book to include a fair number of the milk tanks and their details, which I have been asked for, and also a large selection of containers, which the Great Western Railway sponsored forty years ago, and which, in a more sophisticated form are now the 'latest' thing on British Rail Transport.

In addition, as the few pictures of cranes in the last book seemed to be well received, I have followed these up with a slightly more comprehensive coverage of these fascinating, but unrecorded, machines, not only as breakdown equipment, but also as used for track relaying and goods-loading work.

Much space has been given to the early 'Opens', as it was thought that, although some examples have appeared in various official railway papers, this book would put them in their proper context and also show off the excellence of the vintage camera work. I would add that, for this purpose, the pictures have been produced as large as possible to show the maximum amount of detail, as nothing is more frustrating than trying to deduce small features from tiny illustrations.

Here, then, is another book on those long-departed wagons of the old Great Western Railway Company with the strange sounding names. Who but the Great Western Railway could have thought up such odd appellations as 'Macaw' and 'Gane' for two such similar wagons!

Figure 1

This is an early Swindon picture of open
wagons. Left-hand wagon was of Lot 441 of 1888,
numbers 44201-400, with 16′ overall length
and 9′ wheelbase, originally to Diagram O.5.
Right-hand wagon is an ex-broad-gauge open with
dumb buffers suitable for mixed gauge.

Figure 2

The early bogie open wagon, code name 'Tourn', of
Lot 455 of 1888. It was of 36′ overall
length, with bogies of 4′10″ and wheelbase, at
22′2″ centres. The Diagram was O.1. Note:
one single brake on one bogie only!

Figure 3

Figure 4

A three-plank open wagon, equipped with grease axle boxes and a four-plank open, with sheet supporter, and fitted with oil boxes. Also, note the cattle wagon, with cast name and number plates on the end.

Number 4373 was an example of a single-plank open wagon with a single wooden brake block. The six-wheeled vehicle is a 'Tadpole' ex-broad-gauge fish wagon of 1887, shown as standard gauge wagon stock. Numbers were 42764-99, built to Diagram S.4 or S.5.

Figure 5

Figure 6

Number 11173 is a 'Tadpole' fish wagon, as running on broad gauge. Other numbers were 11174-11208. Converted as in figure 4 and re-numbered, it would have been painted dark grey.

The final form of fish wagon 'Tadpole' taken into the van list, renumbered again to 2009-44 and painted brown with yellow ochre letters, and running on standard gauge.

3

4

Figure 7

Fish bogie wagon, number 2008. This was a one-off vehicle, utilizing the underframe of the old broad gauge Queen's Saloon, and fitted with a new body. Of Lot 1047 of 1904, it was numbered 42809 in the wagon list, but was renumbered 2008 in the van list. Of 33'7½" overall length, 6'4" wheelbase bogie at 20'6" centres, to Diagram S.1.

Figure 8

A fish van of 1909. Built under Lot 625, the numbers were originally 82876-90, renumbered in the passenger van list 2080. 16' overall length, 9' wheelbase, built to Diagram S.2.

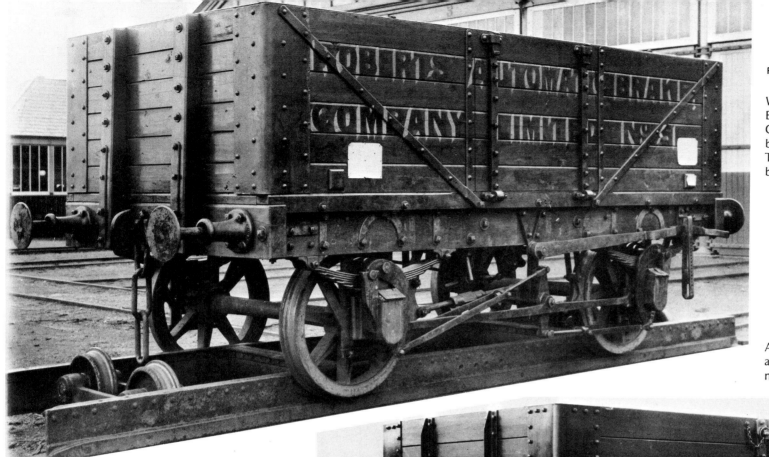

Figure 9

Wagon number 51 of Messrs. Roberts Automatic Brake Company Limited, this was purchased by the Great Western Railway in 1894 for detailed study before embarking on the 'Churchward' brake system. The wagon is shown on the traverser at Swindon with brake gear exposed for record purposes.

A rebuilt four-plank open of the O.5 diagram variety, as photographed at Swindon in 1894. Note the number-plates.

Figure 10

5

The previous brake system was tried out on wagon number 73697 which was of Lot 296 of 1900, also to Diagram O.5. The date on the picture is 1900.

Figure 12

This picture shows wagon number 10793, a four-plank open to Diagram O.5, being used as a prototype mock-up for the 'Churchward' patent brake trials. (This was one system adopted; see page 191 of this book for close-up details.) The photograph is dated 1903.

Figure 11

9

Figure 13

This is a wagon specially constructed for the linoleum traffic. It was of 18′ overall length, with high shaped ends to retain rolls of linoleum, and had a 9′ wheelbase. The vehicle was one of Lot 546 of 1890 to Diagram O.7.

Figure 14

Number 67812, although painted Great Western, was built by private contractors and converted specially for the coal traffic from Fochriw colliery to Fishguard Harbour for the use of the steamers on the Waterford-Rosslare route. The wagon was fitted with end doors for tipping at the Docks. Photograph dated 1922.

The next nine photographs were taken especially in 1902 to illustrate the correct loading techniques for timber etc., via the 'General Appendix' to the *Rule Book of the Great Western Railway*. They are reproduced here as they do show the wagons to advantage. Number 34687 is a three-plank open, fitted with grease boxes and a brake on one side only. Capacity was 8 tons only; Tare weight 4T.12c. Built to Lot 249 of 1882.

Figure 15

Number 45180 is a four-plank open of 10 tons capacity, Tare 5T.0c., and shows the side minus a hand brake. It was built in 1889 of Lot 462 to Diagram O.5. The load is pit props. Figure 16

More pit props, this time loaded into wagon number 19451, a two-plank open with grease boxes and wooden brake blocks. Note the wooden buffer beams. The date was probably 1870.

Figure 17

A four-plank open of 10 tons **capacity**, with a double load of pit props. Tare 4T.17c, number 49108 was built in 1890 of Lot 563 to Diagram O.21.

Figure 18

No. 44600 is carrying a load of sawn timber and is different in that the painted number is on the right and the 'G.W.R.' on the left. The date of the photograph is 1900. This wagon was built in 1888 to Lot 442, to Diagram 0.5.

Figure 19

four-plank opens, three carrying larch poles, and one acting as a check wagon for the overhanging load. Left to right, the numbers are as follows: 52198 Tare 4T.19c, grease box, probably Lot 640, of 1892; 1309 oil box, Lot 202 of 1897, Diagram 0.5; 62782 Tare 5T.2c, grease box, Lot 83 of 1895, Diagram 0.5, 67332, Tare 5T.6c, grease box, Lot 191 of 1897, Diagram 0.5.

Figure 21   This picture shows a sawn timber load with check wagon. Number 64493, a 10-ton, four-plank open, Diagram O.5. Lot 122 of 1895 is acting as check for number 73691, a 10 ton wagon of Tare 5T.9c. Lot 302 of 1900, Diagram O.5. The photograph date is 1901. Number 64493 was built in 1895 to Lot 122, Diagram O.5, and number 73691 was built in 1900 to Lot 302, Diagram O.5.

Figure 20

Figure 21

A picture of number 12325, a five-plank open wagon with a sheet support raised to form a ridge for a tarpaulin wagon sheet. The number of the sheet was Great Western Railway 3562, dated November 1900. The photograph date is March 1909. Lot 447, Diagram 0.5 of 1888.

This is another open wagon fitted with a sheet support bar, but note the low position of the end guides. This seven-plank wagon was number 74778, Lot 456 to Diagram O.2. The picture date is 1905.

Figure 22

Figure 23

Figure 24

This photograph shows the method of using a crow-bar for moving wagons short distances in station yards. The wagon shown is number 45503 with a sheet supporter bar. It was of 10 tons capacity, Tare 5T.3c, and was built in 1889 to Lot 498, to Diagram O.21.

▼ This long overhanging load illustrates the need for a check wagon. These are both four-plank opens; number 1309 has the cast number plates, and number 52198 has painted lettering. The photograph is dated 1902, and the wagons were built in 1892 to Lot 640, and Diagram 0.5.

▼ Ten years on, showing the method of loading bulk timber. Macaw B, number 84149, 30 ton bolster wagon, carries the load, whilst the runner under one end is number 70989. The photograph is dated 1913.

Figure 25

Figure 26

Four-plank open wagon number 54156 is shown loaded with sawn planks, with upright planks to retain the inner load. The capacity of the wagon is 10 tons, Tare weight 4T.17c. It is interesting to note the old track with wooden keys *inside*.

Figure 27

Two ways of transporting floorboards are illustrated on this page. In figure 28 two Mites B, numbers 32139-40, permanently coupled, support the load on their central swivelling bolsters. The capacity of each wagon was 10 tons and the Tare weight of the pair was 10T.1c. The photograph date is 1905. Wagons built to Lot 263 of 1882.

Macaw B number 70897, fully loaded with timber and needing no runner either end. Picture dated 1909. The wagon capacity was 30 tons. Tare 14T.9c. (Figure 29)

Figure 28

Figure 29

Figure 30   20

This picture shows a four-plank open, with sheet support, number 76267, with large 24″ lettering. The date of the photograph is 1907. (Figure 30)

This is a standard four-plank open, with a roped load of rafters longer than the wagon, but not long enough to require a runner. Number 62488 had a Tare weight of 5T.5c, and grease axleboxes. The photograph date is 1908. (Figure 31)

Figure 31

'Crocodile E', number 41948, is carrying a load of a naval launch for the Brazilian Navy, for shipment at the Royal Albert Dock, London, in 1909. The wagon was to Diagram C.15, and was built in 1908. It carried 20 tons with a distributed load, or half that when carrying a central load. (Figure 32)

Figure 32

This photograph shows a heavy German casting being loaded onto a 'Totem' at a South Wales Dockyard in 1910. The wagon number was 41899, originally ex-broad-gauge, and given Diagram B.1. It had a capacity of 45 tons, with a Tare weight of 19T.1c, and measured 37'0" length over buffers, with 5'6" bogies at a 17'6" wheelbase. A drawing of this wagon can be found on page 40 of *A Pictorial Record of Great Western Wagons*, by Jim Russell. Note the stowage of the stanchions along the side. (Figure 33)

Figure 33

Figure 34

Another Continental casting, this time mounted on number 41906 'Crocodile J'. One of two built in 1917—the other being number 41955—the Diagram was C.8, load 50 tons overall, 25 tons in the well. (Figure 34)

A heavy, 41 tons, armour plate roll forms the load for 40 ton capacity 'Crocodile K' in 1908. According to records this should be 'Crocodile G' of 1908, to Diagram C.14, of Lot 596. This weight must have been near the limit for this wagon, as the inscription reads '40 ton load distributed, or half when centrally loaded'. (Figure 35)

Figure 35

An American casting, off-loaded at Cardiff Docks in 1937, is seen on 'Crocodile H', number 41974, which was one of three built in 1926 to Diagram C.23. Others were numbers 41973-75. The load was 65 tons spread, half that in the centre well. (Figure 36)

Figure 36

Figure 37

Another end-tipping wagon, but this one was made at Swindon to Lot 750 of 1913, Diagram O.13, and was constructed for the China clay traffic at Fowey in Cornwall. The overall length was 16', and the wheelbase 9', to carry 12 tons. The Tare weight was 6T.0c. (Figure 37)

Figure 38

Originally built to Lot 518 in 1905, Diagram O.2, with seven-plank 4'3" sides, these opens were rebuilt as shown in 1914, for the conveyance of horses and mules in army service during World War I. Note the rings for tying up the animals. (Figure 38)

Built in 1912 to Lot 798, Diagram O.11, and numbered from 86001 to 87000, some of these wagons were also converted as those in figure 38 for use with military pack-horses and mules. Note the original sheet support guide on the ends. Records show that 400 opens were altered to carry horses and mules in the First World War years. The date of the photograph is 1913. The wagon later became Diagram 0.17.

Figure 39

Figure 40

A vacuum-brake fitted, five-plank open wagon, showing the large 24″ lettering of the 1910 period. Note that the wagon is equipped with either-side ratchet brake, and other 'Churchward' fittings. To carry 10 tons, Tare weight 5T.6c.

A similar wagon to that in figure 22, but forty years on. The photograph was taken by Michael Longridge in 1952, and has retained all the features of the new wagon shown on page 11. (Figure 41)

Figure 41

Figure 42

Yet another five-plank, vacuum-braked, open wagon, built under Lot 912 of 1924, to Diagram O.22. The numbers were 102626-103000, code name 'Opens B' as being fitted with vacuum brake. Note the sloping bottom plank on the side door to throw rainwater from the door lip and save wet-rot at this point. The photograph, dated 1924, was taken for record purposes to show 'non common user' plate. (Figure 42)

Figure 43

A four-plank open, with sheet supporter bar, number 66160, is slightly different in having unusual sheet bar guides at the ends of the wagon, and also non-standard door-stops fixed to the solebar. The latter were not originally fitted, but it was found that the door, crashing open, damaged not only itself but also the brake gear, so these stops were riveted on. They were usually longer and with more spring. Built to Lot 153 of 1897, Diagram O.5.

Figure 44

One of the diagram O.11 series, commandeered by the military in 1914 for service overseas, and fitted with a roof containing hinged bin-doors and divided into three separate compartments. Although painted khaki and numbered 35902, the original Great Western numbering can be seen on the plate (86551). Note that the vehicle is also equipped with screw shackle for Continental railways. Built to diagram O.17 after conversion (Figure 44)

Number 86041, of the same O.11 Diagram as figure 22, seen just before withdrawal in 1952. Several new planks and patches had been added, and a change of ownership to British Rail. The inscription reads 'Empty to Newport (Alexandra Dock Junction)'. (Figure 45)

Figure 45

Figure 46　　Figure 47

A good 'broadside' shot of a 'Mink D' on a moving train, taken by Michael Longridge in 1948. The number is 28909. (Figure 46)

This shows the letter placing and inscriptions on the tall 'Fruit A'. This one is number 59885, and the legend reads 'Empty to Evesham'. (Figure 47)

An official aerial view of the wagon sheet shops at Worcester in 1926. All the wagon tarpaulins (or sheets) were made, repaired, and maintained, at these shops, and dispatched to all stations on the system. Most local goods pick-up trains had an open wagon in their consist, into which sheets could be sent direct to Worcester depot. The wagon numbers on the front siding are 'Ventilated Mink' number 26701, and the four-plank open is number 7685. (Figure 48)

This illustrates the lettering on 'Damo B', number 42227.

Figure 48

Figure 49

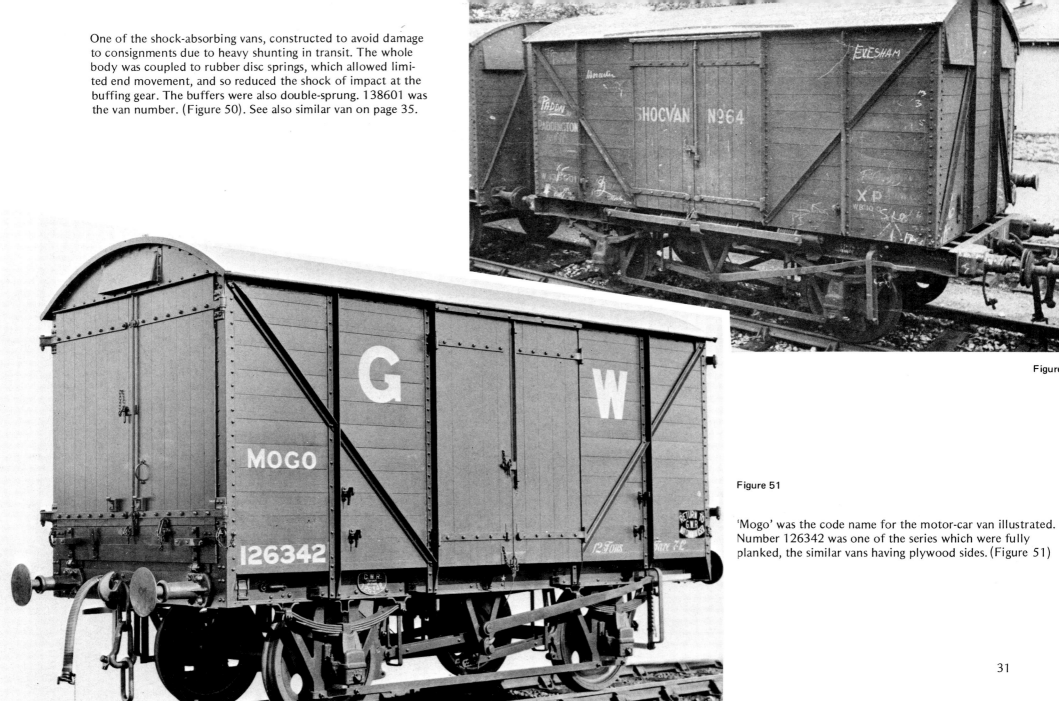

One of the shock-absorbing vans, constructed to avoid damage to consignments due to heavy shunting in transit. The whole body was coupled to rubber disc springs, which allowed limited end movement, and so reduced the shock of impact at the buffing gear. The buffers were also double-sprung. 138601 was the van number. (Figure 50). See also similar van on page 35.

Figure 50

Figure 51

'Mogo' was the code name for the motor-car van illustrated. Number 126342 was one of the series which were fully planked, the similar vans having plywood sides. (Figure 51)

'Goods Fruit A', number 134149, was one of a series built under Lot 1270 of 1938 to Diagram Y.8. The overall length was 17'6", width 8'6.5/8", and wheel-base 10'. Other numbers were 134137-134336.

Figure 53

Forty-four years separate the building dates of this vehicle with that of figure 53. Number 2327 was originally number 47857 of Lot 35, constructed in 1894. The Diagram was Y.2, and the photograph shows the vehicle in the passenger-van list at 1923. Length was 16', wheelbase 10', capacity 6 tons. In the photograph it is painted brown, with yellow ochre letters inscribed 'Return empty to Weymouth'. Note oil lamp in roof. (Figure 52).

Figure 52

Figure 54

One only 'Serpent', built in 1889 to Lot 510 to Diagram G.9. The photograph is dated 1916. (Figure 54)

Roll wagon number 32598. These were originally open wagons rebuilt for carrying heavy rolls or ingots. They were Lot 802 of 1914 to Diagram B.3. The length was 15' over headstocks, 9' wheelbase, capacity 10 tons. The date of the picture is 1914.

Figure 55

One of very early 'Mex' Cattle wagons. Built in 1888 on Lot 433. Numbers were 38100-200 and the Diagram was W.3. Note that only a one sided brake is fitted, and that the wagon is of the 'small' variety.

Figure 56

Figure 57

An official photograph of a shock abosrbing van, taken in 1938 when new, note that the body was free to move longitudinally on the chassis. (Figure 57). See also Figure 50.

EXPERIMENTAL SHOCK ABSORBING VAN No I

G W 12 T 125581

XP NB 10-0 8-12

RETURN TO G.W.R NOT COMMON USER

G.W.R. STANDARD 12 TONS 125581

21-0 8-3

Figure 58

Code name 'Morel', number 42000 was built originally in 1887 to Lot 425, Diagram E.2. It was rebuilt in 1893. Its capacity was just 20 tons, but was later increased to 25 tons. (Figure 58)

Figure 59

This wagon was code named 'Aero', and was for transporting three-bladed aircraft propellers. Built in 1938 to Lot 1314, Diagram E.4, the numbers were 137692-6. Originally rebuilt from flats, they were eventually re-converted to opens in 1950, when their use was no longer needed. (See also page 182).

This photograph of 1909 illustrates wagon number 41999, 'Morel', loaded with a large marine propeller of phosphor-bronze. The capacity of the vehicle was 25 tons, Tare 10T.5c, and it was built in 1909 to Diagram E.3.

Figure 60

Figure 61

Figure 62

One of the first 20 ton capacity all-steel wagons, designed for the transport of coal for the locomotive department. This early version of the 'loco coal' vehicles was fitted with two small drop doors on each side, and had rounded corners. The Diagram was in the N.4 series, and the hand brake was of the crank style, operating on one side only.

Two 20 ton loco coal wagons of Diagram N.4. Figure 64 shows number 53381, an original photograph of 1900, as inscribed for the return empty journey to 'Cilely Colliery', and in figure 63, still going strong, number 53256 is seen under British Rail ownership. The only apparent difference between the two wagons is in the pattern of buffers.

Figure 63

Figure 64

39

A 4 mm drawing of the 20 ton coal wagon, with a plan view showing the rounded corners to the wagon. The dimensions are 20′ over headstocks in length, 7′9″ in width, but 8′2″ over Z irons at the top rim. (Figure 65)

Number 53680 is in the 1930 livery, with the 18″ Great Western lettering. Note that this is a similar wagon to that in figure 64, except that the 'T' irons for the body sides are now on the outside of the body instead of inside, as originally. Built to Lot 424 of 1903, Diagram N.2. (Figure 66)

Figure 65

Figure 66

Figure 67

Another style of 20 ton capacity loco coal wagon is seen in this picture. Again it has an all-steel construction, with 'T' irons outside, but with only one small door on each side, having end doors at both ends instead. (Figure 67)

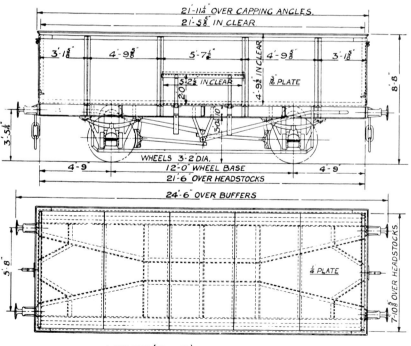

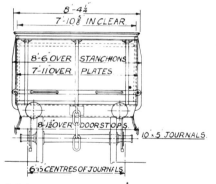

Figure 68

The drawing gives all the dimensions necessary for a good model, and also some information as to Lot numbers, etc. (Figure 68)

CUBICAL CAPACITY ·40·6 CUBIC FT. PER TON.

TARE - 9ᵀ-9ᶜ

—G.W.R.—
—20 TON MINERAL WAGON FOR SOUTH WALES USE—
—METAL BODY, R.C.H. UNDERFRAME & DETAILS—
—SWINDON— —JANUARY— —1924.—

LOT 931.(First 10.)
" 936.
" 937.
" 938.

41

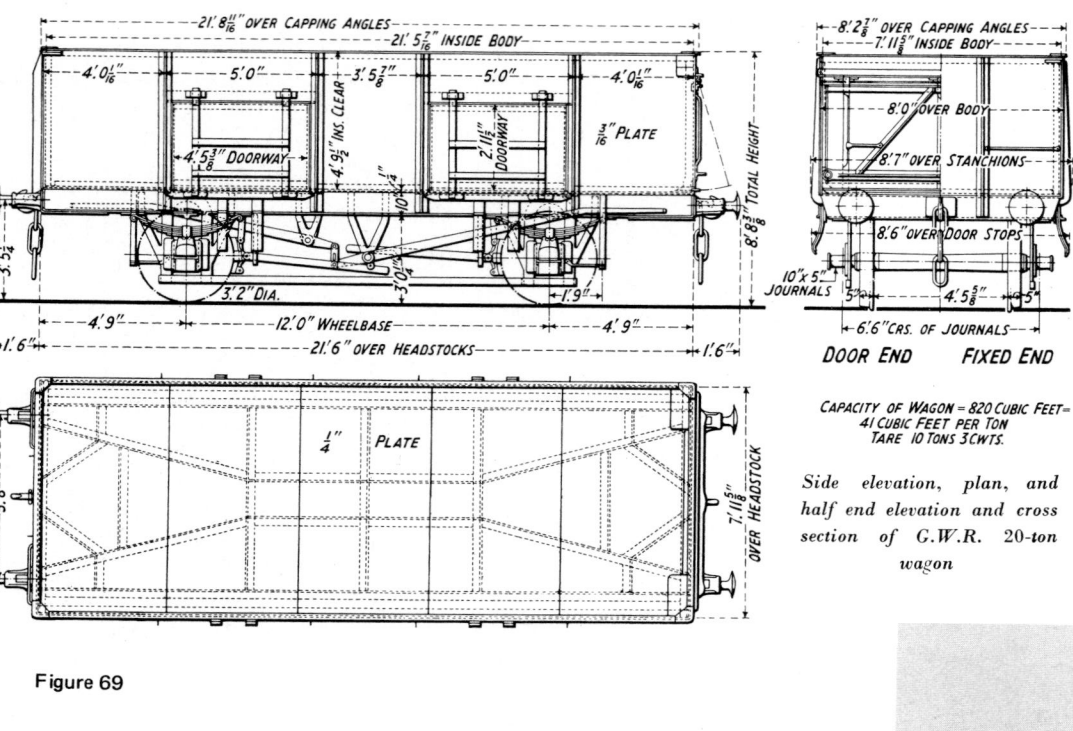

Figure 69

Side elevation, plan, and half end elevation and cross section of G.W.R. 20-ton wagon

Of the same material dimensions as the previous 20 ton coal wagon, this drawing shows the design with one end door and two drop doors on each side. Note that these doors are held in place with drop lugs working in a slot. (Figure 69)

Figure 70

Number 83854 is a similar vehicle in size to that in the drawing, but it has no end doors and the side drop doors are secured by means of a hasp and pin. The photographs were taken during British Rail ownership, and the capacity has been increased to 21 tons. (Figure 70)

Figure 71

Of all-steel construction, number 23886 is a loco-coal wagon of 12 tons capacity. Note the large 24″ lettering of the 'G.W.' and the 9″ 'LOCO'. Painting of these departmental wagons was always black, not the usual grey. Built to Lot 862 of 1920 to Diagram N.20. (Figure 71)

Figure 72

A large 20 ton Hopper wagon, for use with very small coal which could be dropped through a chute in the bottom. The wagon Diagram was N.12, and they were vacuum-braked. Built to Lot 503 of 1905 (Figure 72).

Figure 73

A similar wagon to that in figure 71, of 12 tons capacity, but with slightly different lettering. Note that the word 'LOCO' is of varying size and spacing to that on wagon number 23886, and also that the positioning of the numerals do not exactly relate. (Figure 73)

Figure 74

Of smaller size and capacity, number 23001 is proportionally lower in height, and carries the 18″ lettering. Tare was only 5T.17c, as against the 6T.6c of the 12-tonners. Diagram N.20. Built to Lot 813 of 1915 (Figure 74)

Figure 75

One final example of the N.20 Diagram, 10-ton capacity, loco coal wagon, to show the large 24″ letters which reach right to the top of the vehicle. The date of the photograph is April 1915. (Figure 75)

This shows a round-ended and a square-ended 10-ton example of small loco coal wagons coupled together in service. Figure 77 is of another N.2 Diagram wagon in the same train of coal, heading for the engine sheds. The Locomotive Department always used to collect their coal from the sorting sidings in rakes of wagons like this, and place them on the coaling chutes. The number of the wagon next to the engine is 53584.

Figure 76

Figure 77

Two examples of the new style of lettering adapted in 1904. These wagons have been painted especially for this purpose. Number 53236 is another to Diagram N.4, and the water tank (which was black and white) was for drinking water at outlying depots.

Figure 79

On the same commission as figure 78, this photograph illustrates number 23646, a small wooden four-plank wagon in use as loco coal, and behind is a two-plank open with

A pair of 'Mites' stand first in this picture, permanently coupled at the centre with single pin. Note the hole in the early parallel buffers (for access to the retaining nut!). Number 9631 is a small all-steel loco coal wagon, which has received an extension on the top. ▼

In these painting trials, several styles were tried, and number 53356, Diagram N.2, has the large 24" letters at the extreme ends of the wagon instead of over the doors. The unusual van is one of those used only on the Pontnewynydd branch in South Wales. (See page 125, figure 250, of *A Pictorial Record of Great Western Wagons* for the later version.) (Figure 81)

Figure 80

Figure 81

Number 12009 is a timber-framed brake-van of early vintage. The date on the photograph is 1900, and several points are of interest. Note the brakes are of the wagon type, not clasp, the van still has grease axle boxes, and the frame on the left-hand side is for route diagramming letters. This wagon survived to be Diagram A.A.16. It is 18' overall in length, 11'6" wheel-base, firstly 10 ton, then 12 ton in 1919, and finally 13 tons. (Figure 83)

Figure 83

Figure 82

The Pontnewynydd brake van as built. Note the wet sand-pipe (always straight, not curved!), and the grease boxes fitted. Built in 1889 in Lot 523, the Diagram was A.A.8. They were originally Tare 10T, increased to 12T, and later to 13T. (Figure 82)

Reading Division

P^t WAY   BRAKE

G.W.R   14101

Figure 84

A permanent way construction brake van of 1890. It was built to Lot 531, to Diagram A.A.6, and its length was 20', overall, with 13' wheelbase. Its Tare weight was 13T.10c. Another van of the same lot was number 14794.

Figure 85

One of the early permanent-way brake vans, equipped with a ballast plough. Built in 1893 to Lot 21, they were of 20′ overall length with a 13′ wheelbase. Of interest is the large open verandah, later closed in. The big hand-wheel can be seen fixed to the door partition, by means of which the plough could be lowered onto the rail-head. Notice also the 'P.W.' painted on the end panels and sides. The straight pipes indicate a wet-sand van. (Figure 85)

A close-up of the ballast plough on the P.W. brake van, number 40373, of the same series as figure 85, but in the 1930s. The Diagram of the van was then A.A.5, and it can be seen how the van has been enclosed. Note also the vacuum pipe passing around the top edge of the plough so as to be out of the way of the lifting gear of the latter.

▼

Figure 86

Figure 87

Some doubt has been expressed about the existence of special brake vans for use in tunnels, so this picture should settle the matter. Number 35830 is one such van, originally built in 1889 to Lot 432, and weighing 14 tons. The official photograph, dated 1922, shows the van as Diagram A.A.4, and the tare weight has been increased to 16T. Tunnel vans usually had a drop-light in the door, whereas permanent-way brakes had a two-piece stable door design, with handrails going up to the roof.

One of the ten heavy brake vans built in 1900 and running on six wheels. The numbers were 56975-84. The overall length was 20' with a 6'6" verandah. Wheelbases were 6'6" each. As built and shown in the photograph, the Tare weight was 22T.10c., later increased to 24T, and finally to 25T. The Diagram was A.A.1. Note the cast plates for the number and Company ownership, also notice the brakes on all wheels, and the fact that handrails at this date were not painted white.

Figure 88

Figure 89

An interesting photograph showing the lay-out of the interior of a goods brake van. The guard's chair can be seen on the bottom left, and the equipment lockers on the right. The small coal stove is in the off-centre position, and the sand-boxes can be identified at the end of the van, with the operating gear running along the roof. The three lamps, with which every van was equipped, were two side lamps painted black, with two lenses and slides, and one tail lamp with a red lens, and painted red until just before World War II, when they were changed to white. The paintwork of the van was dark chocolate from floor to waistline, cream above the waist, and a white roof. Other fittings were black.

A page of brake van pictures at various dates, showing number 56931 in 1924, number 56981 in 1947, number 17551 in 1937, and number 56969 in 1952.

▼

Figure 92

Figure 93

Figure 94

Figure 95

Figure 96

Figure 97

Four more Great Western goods brake vans, code name 'Toad'. Long wheelbase, 20 ton, number 114765 seen at Westbourne Park in 1951; 16 ton brake at Bridport, equipped with vacuum and steam heating pipes; Southall brake van, number 35856, dropping on to a train at West Drayton in 1938; Number 56167, 16 ton brake van branded 'Oxley Sidings' at Paddington Goods Depot in 1935.

Figure 98

An unusual Great Western van. The underframe seems to be of Swindon manufacture, but the body—is it ex South Wales? It could almost be L.N.E.R. (Figure 98)

▲

Figure 99

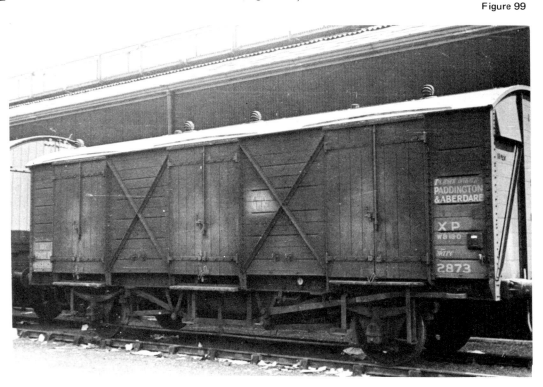

▲

One of the 18′ wheelbase 'Fruit D' vans seen at Paddington goods; a 'brown' vehicle but often seen in freight trains as well as passenger trains. Number 2873 is branded 'To work between Paddington and Aberdare'. These vans were often used for parcels traffic. (Figure 99)

Although branded 'Bogie Bolster', this vehicle, number 17331, was one of the ex W.D. vehicles, used on the Great Western Railway and converted with the addition of bolsters and stanchions to carry loads as shown. They were known on the Great Western Railway as 'Rectank'. (Figure 100)

57

Figure 100

This print illustrates the 'Rectank' as hired to the Great Western Railway for its original purpose, namely the carriage of Army tanks. Numbers in this style were 212005, 212080/1/2/9/94/5, 212112/5/20, 212107/8. Note the screw jacks under the cross bearers for relieving the weight whilst loading.

Figure 101

Figure 102

A special van for the carriage of gunpowder and explosives. The photograph is dated 1939. The Diagram is Z.4 to Lot 1346. It had an unusual capacity of 7 tons. The painting was black with light grey roof; the G.P.V. and diagonal stripes in red. Code name 'Cone'. Other lettering, white.

Figure 103

A gunpowder van, improvised from Iron Mink ex Diagram V.6, and hired to the Southern Railway. The date of the photograph is March 1938. Great Western Railway code name 'Cone'.

Number 41905 is seen conveying a marine propeller at Cardiff Docks in 1947. The original vehicle was built in 1901 under Lot 219 as 'Crocodile E', Diagram C.7, and was rebuilt in 1910 and again in 1939 for propellers and classed as 'Crocodile A'. Others in the series were numbers 41904 and 41906.

Figure 104

Figure 105

62

An early picture of a 'Crocodile A'. To Lot 606 of 1892, it was originally number 36882, and finally was converted to 'Crocodile C'. 50′ length over headstocks, 31′ in well, 4′6″ bogies at 40′6″ centres. Note the broad gauge stock in the background. (Figure 105)

'Crocodile C', photographed in 1939, was originally 'Crocodile G' of Lot 516 of 1906. Numbers 41929–32 were rebuilt in 1910 to carry 15 tons in the well. Size 52′ over headstocks, 31′2″ in well. Built to Diagram C.4. (Figure 106)

Figure 106

Figure 107

These two pictures illustrate an interesting adaptation of a Great Western 'Crocodile'. The pictures, taken at Swindon in 1915, show numbers 41976 and 41977 converted as mobile 6″ gun platforms. Outriggers were fitted which could be run out on both sides and a platform let down on to these bearers, forming a large area for a gun to traverse. Figure 107 shows the vehicle with outriggers stowed, and in figure 108 they are ready for action, with clips on the railhead. The Diagram was probably C.8, converted to C.9. There is no record of these two wagons being returned to the Great Western Railway, in fact number 41977 was later used for 'Crocodile L'.

Figure 108

Figure 109

Especially for modellers, this view shows the interior of the 'well' of number 42020. The bearers were movable in a lengthways direction to accommodate varying loads. The picture was taken in the special wagon yard at Swindon.

Of 1938 vintage, the 'Crocodile M' series was built to Lot 1298 to Diagram C.28. It was a long vehicle, 62'6" overall length, with 41'6" clear in well, fitted with 5'6" bogies at 52' centres. The numbers were 42020-4. (Figure 110)

Figure 110

Figure 111

A passenger cattle box, code name 'Beetle C', built in 1927 under Lot 1386 to Diagram W.7. There were ten in the order, numbers 200/3/5/6/10/14/16/19/20/22. They were 26′ overall length with 16′ wheelbase, and came on the passenger van list, being 'brown' vehicles. Note the 'G.W.' on the ends.

An interesting shot of the 'one-off' number 41977 'Crocodile L', illustrating its ability to accept sharp radii curves. The Diagram was C.25 of Lot 1042, built in 1930. (Figure 112)

Figure 112

Figure 113

A 12,500 K.V.A. transformer made by the Hack-
bridge Electric Co. loaded on to a 'Crocodile G'
No. 36950.

A massive stator made by Metro-Vickers of Trafford
Park, loaded on the one only 120 ton 'Crocodile L.'
in 1931. Weight of load 73 tons.

Figure 114

Figure 115

Two large girders made by Messrs. Horsehay & Co.
of Salop, loaded on to 'Crocodile E' No. 41958 with
two container flats running as check wagons.

Figure 116

Single girder loaded on to two boiler wagons 'Pollen B' Nos. 48981-82. (Figure 116)

Figure 117

Figure 117 shows the second girder which made up the train in Figure 115.

Figure 118   70

A conversion of an old 'Siphon' chassis of 1931, number 39882 is a six-wheel wagon rebuilt for conveying varnish from the I.C.I. works at Slough in 1947. Lot number was 1604, and the Diagram was E.E.2. Its length was 27'4½" over-all, with a wheelbase of 9'6" X 9'6", and it carried four tanks, each with a capacity of 500 gallons. Note how the tanks are slightly tilted so that varnish would not seize up the outlets when the tanks were empty. (Figure 118)

This is a similar conversion; an old 'Fruit' chassis has been used as a tank support for the transport of acid for the Locomotive dept. (Figure 119)

Number 43976 is another vehicle of different style, but used for the purpose of a tender to crane testing truck. Lot 19 of 1893, Diagram K.2. (Figure 120)

Figure 119

Figure 120

Figure 121

This is a single-tank vehicle for the transport of gas from the plant at Swindon to outlying depots, to supply coaches for lighting. Number 21 had the chassis made by the Carriage and Wagon Dept., and the tank by the Locomotive Shops. No diagram or Lot numbers are known; the photograph is dated 1895. (Figure 121)

Number 32 is a multi-tank gas storage wagon to Diagram D.D.4. The building date is about 1896. Note the shape of the buffer beams which shows that it is of an early vintage. The photograph is dated 1918 at Swindon. The wheelbase is 12'0", width overall 8'11", tanks 8'1". The hand brake was on one side only. (Figure 122)

Figure 122

Figure 123

Figure 124

Wagon number 3, code name 'Cordon', is a gas tank with two cylinders. Note the slightly raised platform at the rear. The photograph, dated 1949, was taken at Old Oak Common. The dimensions on the vehicle are 22'8" × 8'6", and wheelbase is 9'. (Figure 123)

A single cylinder tank, number 12, used also for the conveyance of gas, photographed at Swindon in 1952. The dimensions on the vehicle are 28'2" × 8'2", Tare weight 14T.7c. (Figure 124).

A similar gas tank to number 3, this one is pictured at Banbury station in 1952. The number 17 is at the opposite end to that in figure 123. The Tare weight is 11T.10c, and the dimensions on the vehicle are 22'6" × 8'10", with a 9' wheelbase. (Figure 125)

Loco Dept. Oil tank wagon, number 43983, as seen at Tyseley in 1950. It had a Tare weight of 8T.17c. and a capacity of 3108 gallons. Built to Lot 108 of 1896, Diagram D.D.7.
Number 43979, a similar tank to figure 126, again built to Diagram D.D.3, but with a different tank top filler. Tare weight 9T.8c. Photographed at Swindon in 1952. Built to Lot 222 of 1898.

Figure 125

Figure 128

Gas tank number 22, another single cylinder vehicle similar to that in figure 121; the two pictures show both sides of the wagon. The photograph was taken at Old Oak Common in 1949, and the inscription on the tank reads 'WEST LONDON GAS DEPOT'. Dimensions of the wagon are 32'6" X 7'6", Tare weight 15T.

Figure 129

Figure 130

74

This is an official photograph, dated 1916, of Oil tank wagon number 43939, and was used for conveying inflammable liquid. It was built in 1901 under Lot 335 to Diagram D.D.3. The painting was white with a dark red band and red letters, black underframe. Wheelbase 12'0". Tare weight 8T.15c.

This shows a drinking-water tank for use at outlying depots with no access to drinking water; it was always replenished at Swindon. Built in 1948 under Lot 1551 to Diagram D.D.7, its length was 23'11" overall, wheelbases 6'6" × 6'6", width 7'9". The tank was 14'11¼" × 7'4" diameter, and had a 2000 gallon capacity. (Figure 131). Painted black & white.

Figure 131

Figure 132

Number 2003 was built in 1927 of Lot 1387 to Diagram O.23. It started life as a four-wheel vehicle, but changed later to six wheels, (then Diagram 0.44). The painting details are: aluminium tank, black chassis with white letters. The dimensions of the vehicle are 21′5″ × 7′8″, wheelbase 10′6″ Tare weight 11T.6c.

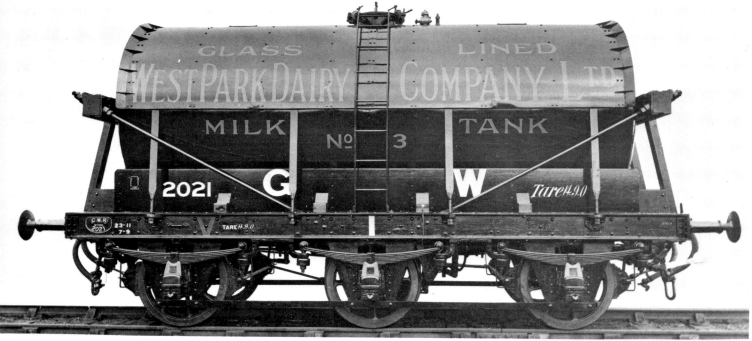

A later style of milk tank, built under Lot 1473 in 1931 to Diagram O.35. The painting is said to have been: brown tank with yellow letters, chassis as figure 132. Dimensions on wagon were 23′11″ × 7′9″, Tare weight 14T.9c. (Figure 133)

Figure 133

Figure 134

Milk tank number 2073 at Swindon in 1952 to Diagram O.36. (Figure 134)

Figure 135

Milk tank number 2507 at Swindon in 1952, to Diagram O.38. The small plate on the right hand side reads 'UNITED DAIRIES'. Originally the milk tank traffic started in 1927. United Dairies opened a depot at Wootton Bassett, and in London at Mitre Bridge.

Figure 136

Milk tank number 2516, also at Swindon in 1952, to Diagram O.39. The aluminium tank is lettered 'U.D.'. Many firms used this form of transport for milk, working between Whitland and London, Addison Road. Also Hemyock, Yetminster, Frome and Lavington, to London.

Milk tank number 2002, same station and date as figure 136 to Diagram O.44. (Figure 137)

Figure 137

Figure 138

Milk tank number 1959 at Swindon in 1952, to Diagram O.52. The tank is painted M.M.B. number 105 (Milk Marketing Board).

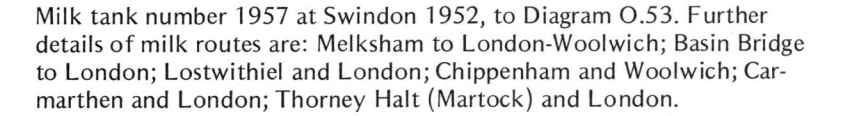

Milk tank number 1957 at Swindon 1952, to Diagram O.53. Further details of milk routes are: Melksham to London-Woolwich; Basin Bridge to London; Lostwithiel and London; Chippenham and Woolwich; Carmarthen and London; Thorney Halt (Martock) and London.

Figure 139

Figure 140

This milk tank at Swindon in 1952 was wagon number 1991, built to Diagram O.55. It had a 13'0" (6'6" × 6'6") wheelbase and a Tare weight of 13T.12c. All milk tanks were the property of the Milk Company, the chassis belonging to the Railway Company. (Figure 140)

Milk tank number 3033. The plate reads 'UNITED DAIRIES'. The wagon was to Diagram O.57, and the capacity of the tank was 3000 gallons. It weighed 4 tons when empty, 18 tons when loaded fully.

Figure 141

Figure 142

This is an official photograph of number 2022, a milk tank for the Express Dairy, built in 1931 to Lot 1473, to Diagram O.35. The tank was painted navy blue with white letters; the railway chassis was black and white as usual. Dimensions 23'11" × 7'9". Several of these tanks had a sun shade false top which covered the top half of the tank and allowed a stream of air to flow and help in cooling. This can be seen in this picture, however spilt milk soon smells, and the covers just had to go!

Wagon number 2503 was a six-wheeled vehicle for the transport of road milk tank trailers on their own wheels. It was built in 1932 under Lot 1485, to Diagram O.37. The dimensions on the wagon are 23'11" × 8'6". Tare weight 11T.11c. (Figure 143)

Figure 143

Figure 144

Milk tank number 2543 on hire to the C.W.S. It was painted dark green and lettered in white; it is reported that others were signal red with gold lettering, but no proof exists. Built in 1935 to Diagram O.38, under Lot 1543. (Figure 144)

This is a twin-tank milk wagon, number 2552. Built in 1935 under Lot 1548, the Diagram was O.41. These could have been the red tanks with gold lettering mentioned in previous figures.

Figure 145

Figure 146

Another six-wheeled wagon for road tanks, number 2936 was built in 1931 under Lot 1470, Diagram O.45, which was slightly larger than Diagram O.37. The dimensions on the wagon are 27'11" X 8'6". Tare weight 12T.12c. (Figure 146)

Wagon number 2563 was a navy blue and white milk tank with 'Staybrite' inner. It was built in 1935 to Lot 1561, to Diagram O.42. Its dimensions were 23'11" X 7'9", Tare weight 12T.12c. (Figure 147)

Figure 147

One of the first road milk tank trailers for use on the 'Rotank' wagons. This large trailer was painted red with gold lettering, and ran on solid tyres; later trailer tanks were fitted with pneumatic tyres. (Figure 148)

Figure 148

End plan view of the loading and holding gear on the 'Rotank' wagons. This vehicle, number 1731, was photographed in 1949, and worked with the Guinness Company's road tanks conveying stout. (Figure 149)

Figure 149

83

Figure 150   Two descriptive pictures to illustrate clearly how the loading on of milk
trailers was accomplished. Note the stop chock on the wagon, to
prevent over-run. It perhaps should be mentioned that, as the trailer ran
on to the wagon, smaller diameter steel wheels engaged on the sloping
ramp and relieved the weight off the pneumatic tyres whilst in transit.

Operating pulleys and guides can be clearly seen in this picture for
left-hand or right-hand use. The pulley wheel just to the right of the
figure 12 (Tare weight) was loose, and could move side to side on a
pivot pin. Heavy shackles can be seen, which coupled on to U-shackles
on the milk tank. The wagon number in both pictures is 2501.

Figure 151

Figure 152

Wagon number 2503 is seen loaded with a road milk tank trailer at Swindon in 1952. It is interesting to compare this photograph with figure 154, taken after approximately 20 years' interval. (Figure 152).

An end on view of a loaded trailer, shackled up and ready for the journey. Note how pneumatic tyres are clear of the wagon deck. Also note the hinged fall plate of the right-hand buffer, so these wagons standing together could have one plate each to form a bridge over the buffers for loading or off-loading. (Figure 153)

85

Figure 153

Figure 154

Wagon number 2501 again, shown loaded and cleared away ready for being marshalled into its train. The photograph was taken in 1932. Note the cross chains and end shackles. (Figure 154)

A war-time milk tank belonging to the Milk Marketing Board. The wagon number is 1963. Dimensions on the wagon: 23'11" X 7'9", Tare weight 13T.8c. Photographed at Swindon in 1944. (Figure 155)

Figure 155

Figure 156

87

'Rotank' vehicles at the London Wholesale Dairies depot, Wood Lane, illustrating the method of emptying the tank by a flexible pipe, straight into the dairy. A stack of 10-gallon churns has been arranged to show the comparison of the capacity of both tank and churns. The date of the picture is 1935.

Figure 157

88

One of the last milk tank wagons built under the aegis of the Great Western Railway, number 3027, to diagram O.58, is of the two-compartment type contained within one skin, as can be seen by the two filler orifices and double ladders. The dimensions on the wagon are 23'11" X 7'9", weight 13T.14c. The date of the photograph is 1947.

The final milk tank which is actually for conveying liquid for 'Independent Milk Suppliers'. Still carrying the Great Western Railway number plates on which the G. & R. have been blacked out, this is wagon number 3057. The picture is dated May 1948. The dimensions on the wagon are 23′ 11″ X 7′ 9″, Tare weight 141.9c. Single compartment tank. Wagon to Diagram O.56.

Figure 158

Two pictures illustrating the first use of containers, namely house removals. Note the chocolate and cream livery. (Figures 159 & 160)

Figure 159

Figure 160

Figure 161

There were many types of containers used on the Great Western between the wars, and as they have seldom been mentioned in print, I am trying to rectify that here on the next few pages. Two are shown here, both of the BK series—numbers 1869 and 1872, painted chocolate brown with yellow markings and grey roofs—are seen loaded onto 'Conflats' numbered 39063 and 39206, 12-tonners, Tare weight 5T.15c. Note the spring-loaded shackles. (Date 1932-3)

Container BC. 1710 was used for conveying cycles or other merchandise. Load 4 tons, Tare weight 2T.3c. Wagon number 39326 'Conflat', dimensions 20'11" X 8'0", Tare weight 5T.12c.

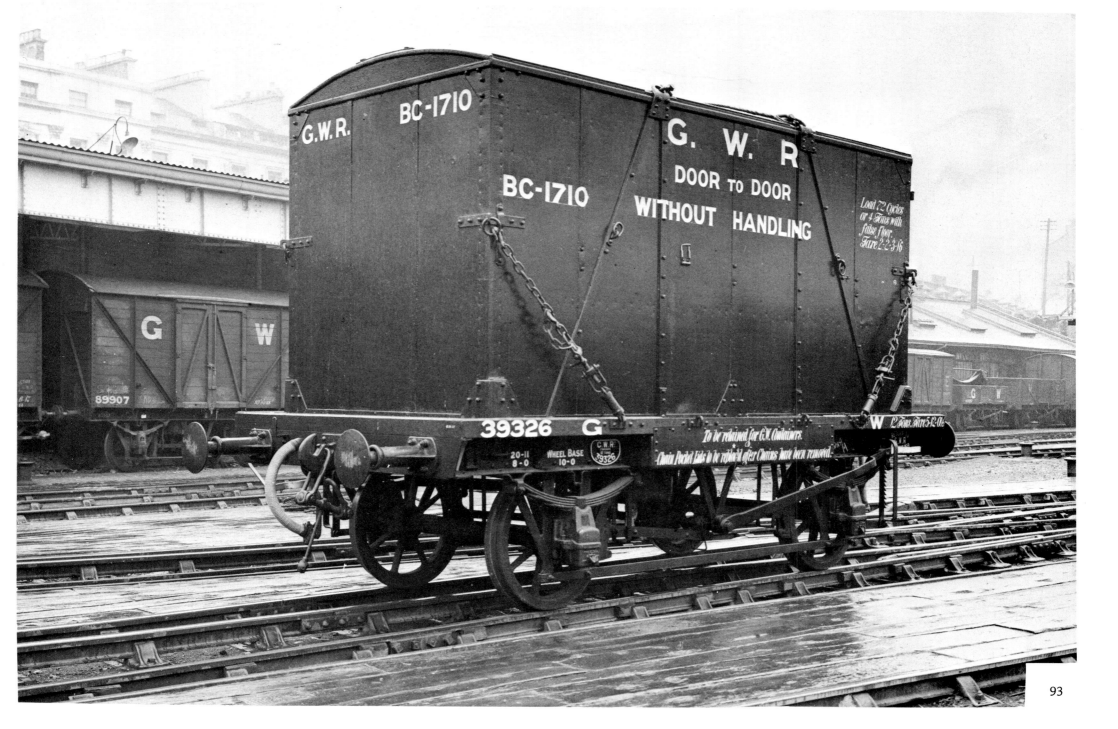

93

Figure 163

Insulated container number FX.1625 was photographed at Penzance in 1936, loaded with bulbs for Manor Farm, Marazion. Note the ice-boxes in the roof. Painted white with black lettering The fish van 'Bloater' in the background is number 2198.

Another insulated container, number FX. 1214, photographed in 1938 on 'Conflat' number 39354. Eight iron bars were fixed across the container with six swivel hooks per bar for hanging meat inside. Diagram F.X.1. of 1932.

Figure 164

Number 39244 'Conflat', loaded with Container FX.1626, painted white with black lettering. The Diagram was FX.1 and dimensions were 14′5″ × 6′6″ × 7′8″. Pictured at Park Royal in 1935 loaded with meat. The sides, ends, roof and floor were double-cased with insulation between.

Figure 165

A 1935 photograph of furniture container number K.1709, loaded on wagon number 39408 at Paddington Goods shed in 1935. The container is to Diagram K.1, serial numbers K.1347-1521, 1672-1721. Its size was 15′2¼″ × 7′0″ × 8′0″. The original colouring was cream above the waistline, brown below, with black lettering; later, as in the picture, they were

K-1709

GWR

K-1709

K-1709
FURNITURE REMOVAL SERVICE
4 Tons. Tare 14 0 4 20
WITH CHEAP TRAVEL FACILITIES
GWR
ESTIMATES
FREE

G
20752

G
W 12 Tons. Tare 5 5 1 20
39408
To be returned for G.W. Containers. 617
Chain Pocket Lids to be replaced after Chains have been removed.
WHEEL BASE 10-0 20-11 8-0
G.W.R. STANDARD 12 TONS 39408
G.W.R.

A 1936 photograph of merchandise container type B.1788, painted red ▲ with yellow letters. Its dimensions were 15'8½" length inside, 6'6¾" width inside, 6'0½" in clear end doors, 5'0" clear side doors, outside dimensions 16'5" × 7'5" × 7'10¾". This is wagon number 39612 of Lot 1188 of 1936, to Diagram H.7.

A small open container for the transport of tiles and other ceramics, ▶ packed in straw. Type D.324, on wagon 39754. Diagram D.1. Photographed at Old Oak Common in 1939.

Figure 168

This ventilated meat container of the H series, number 1086, was of ▶
all-steel construction with a capacity of 4 tons. Painted white with
black lettering, it is on 'Conflat' number 39001, which was of 12 tons
capacity, Tare 5T.18c. The photograph is dated 1937. Ventilation was
assisted by means of space in the roof. (Figure 168)

B series container for conveying paint and varnish in cans; number 164,
to carry 4 tons. Date 1930. On Match truck number 32804 of 10 tons
capacity, Tare 4T.10c. (Diagram B.1.) (Figure 169)

99

Figure 169

Figure 170

FX container number 1622, showing the blank end with no doors and ice-box on the roof, with the lid open. Of wooden construction outside, it was painted white all over, with black letters. Its capacity was 4 tons.

A photograph of the same container as in figure 170, but showing the end with double sealing doors and the roof ice-box lid in a closed position. Note that the door fastenings are similar to those on the 'Mica' wagons. The Tare weight of the container is 1T.15c. Photograph dated 1934.

Figure 171

Figure 172

The K series of furniture container were steel-sided, with wooden top doors. Number 1709 is seen after coming straight from the paint shop at Swindon. Painted brown, with yellow lettering, its capacity was 4 tons with a Tare weight of 1T.10c.

To carry 4 Tons
Tare 14·3·27

GWR

B-2179

DOOR
TO
DOOR
CONTAINER
TRANSPORT

GWR
B-2179

An all-steel construction container of the B series, used for general merchandise transport. Ribs are pressed into the body sides and doors to give added strength. The paint details are: brown body, yellow letters, grey roof. Photograph dated 1938.

Figure 173

Figure 174

Painted white with the usual black lettering, this container is one of the M series, number 1101. It is liberally ventilated even with 'ash' vents in the roofs of the coaching stock type. This container is seen loaded on to 'Conflat' number 39230. Date of photograph, 1935.

Figure 175

This small container of 1T. 13c capacity is seen being loaded in Paddington Goods Depot in 1934. Of the C.C. series the number was 413. Being of the hopper type, doors were fitted into the bottom. I like the early diesel-electric crane with solid tyres.

Figure 176

The loading of a large container in a goods yard, again by means of a mobile crane similar to the one in figure 175. This view of the crane shows the rear and opposite side to that on previous page. The capacity of the crane was 2 tons, and it was manufactured by Ransomes. The wagon in the picture is Match truck 32056. The container is of an early variety with a large 'G.W.R.' on the sides, its number is undecipherable. Photograph dated 1928.

This picture, taken in 1927, is of a fixed yard crane loading a small padlocked container onto an L.M.S. lorry. (On hire perhaps?)

Figure 177

Figure 178

A diagonally planked container, BP.1722, was used for merchandise loaded at Bristol and is branded to be returned there when empty. This picture shows the end without doors, with just two small louvred ventilators at the top. The painting would again be of the brown body and yellow lettering style.

This Ransomes 2-ton mobile crane is loading one of the B series containers onto an old Thorneycroft lorry at Paddington goods. The container number is 88, with number 105 still in the wagon behind. Note that the lorry is painted chocolate and cream.

Figure 179

Figure 180

The same design of container as in figure 178, BP.1722, illustrates the opposite end with the double doors. Note that this type of container does not have the drop-down bottom flap to the doors, but is of the full-length swing pattern. The capacity was only 1T.10c, Tare weight 14c.2q.

Figure 181

Number 669 is another of the 'D' pattern open containers for the carriage of tiles, pipes, and similar fragile items. Note that in this style the ends can be let down, and the sides lifted out, to facilitate loading and unloading. (Figure 181)

This small all-steel hopper container is of the 'G' design for the carriage of grain, or other merchandise if necessary. The corrugations on the sides are for strength. The whole top was either hinged or there was a small trap door in the top side; also one end was removable. The load was 2½ tons of grain or 4 tons of goods. (Figure 182)

Figure 182

111

Figure 183

112

Figure 183 (H1204) was a really small container for the carriage of heavy but fragile merchandise but with little volume. The 'H' series could be moved about on a two-wheeled handcart. Colour scheme was brown with yellow ochre letters.

Figure 184

This picture shows a cement hopper container of 1947 a few months before nationalization. With this welded steel construction the interior was quite smooth, allowing the cement or similar fluid material to be loaded through the trap in the roof, and deposited on site by means of the drop door in the bottom which was released by the lever at the side. The capacity was 3½ tons, or 90 cubic feet, and the Tare weight was ½T. Type and number BB.2952, body painted bauxite with white letters.

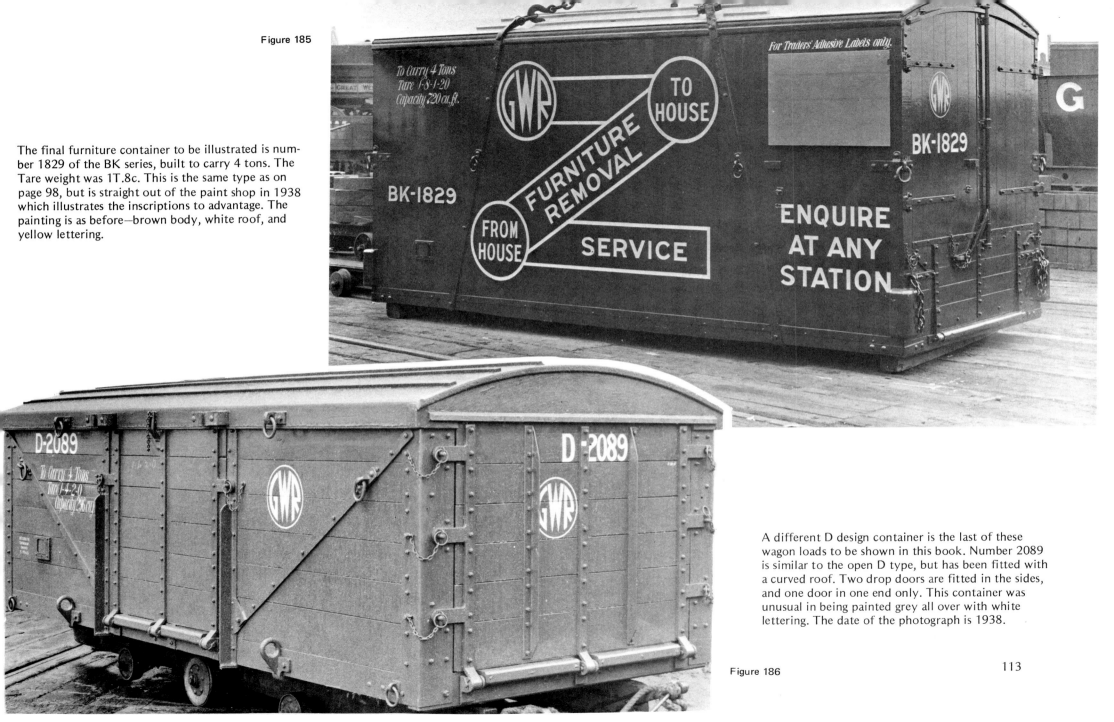

Figure 185

The final furniture container to be illustrated is number 1829 of the BK series, built to carry 4 tons. The Tare weight was 1T.8c. This is the same type as on page 98, but is straight out of the paint shop in 1938 which illustrates the inscriptions to advantage. The painting is as before—brown body, white roof, and yellow lettering.

A different D design container is the last of these wagon loads to be shown in this book. Number 2089 is similar to the open D type, but has been fitted with a curved roof. Two drop doors are fitted in the sides, and one door in one end only. This container was unusual in being painted grey all over with white lettering. The date of the photograph is 1938.

Figure 186

113

Figure 187

114

This is one of the earliest shunter's trucks known to me. Originally built as an open (number 10235 B.G.) by Hennett in 1854 for the South Devon Railway, it passed into the Great Western Railway eventually converted as shown, and was stationed at Exeter in 1884. The photograph is dated 1888, and one can see the dumb buffers which are extended sideways to allow shunting with mixed gauge stock. (Figure 187)

Number 41834 was a special shunter's truck, built for work at Morpeth Dock, Birkenhead. First constructed under Lot 189 of 1897 (to Diagram M.), it is completely different from the usual pattern of Great Western shunting trucks. Similar vehicles were built at Crewe for the L.N.W./G.W. joint lines. (Figure 188)

Figure 188

Figure 189

Figure 190

Two pictures of the same vehicle, a standard Swindon-made shunting truck built to Diagram M.1 of Lot 77 in 1895. The date of photographs is April 1896. It is interesting to note the use of grease axle-boxes, the hornplates sheeted in to prevent shunters accidentally putting their poles into the wheel spokes. There is one brake on one side only. Number 41898 was for use at Cardiff.

Figure 191

116

Shunter's truck number 41808, earmarked for one of Banbury's marshalling yards (of which there used to be six!). This wagon was built in 1900, to Diagram M.1, under Lot 315, and the photograph was taken in April 1922. The wagons were painted Great Western grey all over, with white letters. (Figure 191)

A later design, fitted with vacuum pipe, but not brake, was number 41054, shown new in 1937. Built under Lot 1261, the Diagram was M.4. Several differences can be seen between the two types, especially in hand-rails and stanchions.

Figure 192

Figure 193

Two shunting trucks used by Passenger shunters at Old Oak Common carriage sidings. Both pictures were taken by Mike Longridge in 1952 and they show the same design, but the lower wagon has been fitted with a through vacuum pipe with the upper fitting. In Great Western days this pipe would have been painted red to indicate that it was only a through pipe. Note that these wagons carry lamp brackets to suit loco headlamps, for if the wagon was being propelled then loco headlamps would be attached. Conversely there was also provision for a traffic dept. tail lamp.

Figure 194

Figure 195

Number 41713 'Coral A' was shown in *A Pictorial Record of Great Western Wagons* by Jim Russell, but the picture was taken from a reproduction. On this original print the detail can be seen much clearer. Built to Lot 141 in 1899 to Diagram D.2, the photograph shows the wagon as new. Its dimensions were 21'6" overall, 17'6" in clear, with a 12' wheelbase. To carry 12 tons, Tare weight 7T.4c. (Figure 195)

Of the same dimensions as number 41713, this wagon, number 41722, was built ten years later, in 1909, under Lot 583. The Diagram was still D.2, and its code name 'Coral A', but the photograph was not taken until 1941. Note the disc wheels. (Figure 196)

Figure 196

The grain wagon shown in *A Pictorial Record of Great Western Wagons* caused much comment and speculation, so I have included this photograph to show how the interior and floor were arranged. There were iron flaps inside, which could be dropped down onto the floor when the vehicle was being used as a covered goods van. (Figure 197)

A self-explanatory picture, illustrating the method of loading these wagons with grain through the roof hatch. These grain hoppers were made in 1929 under Lot 1006 to Diagram V.20, and there were twelve numbers 42232-43. The dimensions were 21'6" overall, 10'6" wheelbase, 20 tons capacity, Tare weight 12T.7c. Discharging could be accomplished by a suction pipe through the top hatch or through the bottom doors into a chute or belt conveyor. It was used by Cobden Flour Mills Ltd. between Wroxham and Birkenhead. (Figure 198)

Figure 198

Figure 199

120

This early vehicle is one of many which were built between 1879 and 1881. Some were as covered vans and others, like this one, were for conveying meat. The numbering started at 29000 and worked backwards. Two specific Lots were for meat vans—namely, Lot 169 of 1879, numbers 28940-28916, and Lot 230 of 1881, numbers 28915-28866. It is thought that number 28657 was probably one of Lot 321 of 1884—the picture is dated 1894. Notice the water tank slung under the chassis.

Figure 200

The same vehicle as in figure 199, but showing more detail at the end. It would appear that the very early method of cooling was to fit two layers of wire mesh with some absorbent material sandwiched between, and then, by means of the hand-pump mounted on the end, water was pumped up from the tank in the underframe to the roof, and allowed to seep down through the open mesh sides, so giving a measure of cooling. Note the early form of Great Western Railway axlebox. The photograph is dated 1894.

Figure 201

122

This was the original design of a ventilated meat van. Number 47951, shown as built in 1889, was to Lot 490 and to Diagram X.1. Other numbers on the Lot were 47901-48000. The dimensions were 16′ overall length with a 10′ wheelbase, and the Tare weight was 7T.17c, with a capacity of 6 tons. The vehicle was fitted with Mansell coach wheels and Dean vacuum brake gear, and, as it was permitted to run in passenger trains, note the side-lamp brackets at each end. Painting would be grey all over with white letters. Code name 'Mica'.

Figure 202

Code name 'Mica A', this van was constructed for the conveyance of chilled meat from London Docks to South Wales, as can be seen by the inscription. Ice containers were installed inside and, together with lots of straw for insulation, the carcases were rushed from Victoria Dock to Cardiff. Construction was of double diagonal planking with one small door. Fitted with a through vacuum pipe, the wagon could be attached to passenger trains but was not braked as such. Painting details were: white body, with red lettering and black underframe. Date of picture—March 1903. Diagram X.3. (Ex South Wales)

123

Also photographed in 1903, this example of a 'Mica B' illustrates a further development in the meat wagon design. The vehicle had a dual role; with the ventilators open at the ends it could be used as an ordinary meat van, or with the addition of ice and vents closed, the wagon could then become a refrigerator, for frozen or chilled meat. Fitted with wagon wheels, but also equipped with vacuum brake, it could be worked on both freight or passenger trains if necessary. The paintwork was white with red letters, black underframe and white roof. Capacity 6 tons, Tare weight 8T.11c. Built to Diagram X.2 of Lot 152 of 1897.

Figure 203

...similar vehicle to that shown in figure 203, number 59761 is one of a series built in 1903 under Lot 420 to Diagram X.2. There were ninety constructed on this order, numbering from 59701 to 59790. Dimensions were 16′ overall length with a 10′ wheelbase; to carry 6 tons with a Tare weight of 8T.11c. Note that by now (1904) the new style of lettering is being used. Paintwork on this wagon was unusual in that the body and roof were white with red letters, but the whole chassis was painted dark grey, with the exception of the vacuum pipe which was black!

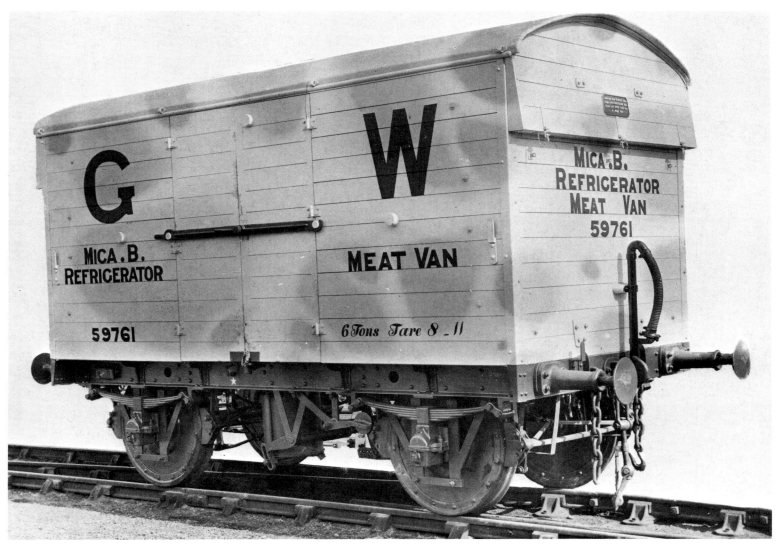

Figure 204

125

Figure 205

126

This picture was taken in 1934, which shows the small 18″ lettering 'G.W.' in white on a dark grey body and chassis, with a white roof. Number 59791 was built in 1903 under Lot 429, again to Diagram X.2. The design was for a meat van, ventilated, but provision was made for the installation of ice-boxes if needed. Other numbers were 59792-800. Note that a step has been provided for access to the doors from track level. Dimensions on the wagon were 19′8″ X 8′1″; load 6 tons, Tare weight 8T.7c.

Figure 206

As the meat traffic dwindled, so the need for a large number of meat vans declined, and in 1938 many 'Micas' and 'Micas B' were converted to 'specific purposes', amongst which was the carriage of tea from Messrs. Lyons of Greenford's premises for shipment at Birkenhead (see Vol. I). The wagon illustrated was originally built in 1930 under Lot 1035 as a 'Mica' to Diagram X.9, and was converted to 'Tevan' in 1938, the date of the photograph. The Diagram then became V.31 of the covered van series. Paintwork was the usual white with red letters. Dimensions on van—20'11" X 8'1", Tare 8T.13c. Underframe black.

Figure 207

128

This old 'Mica B' had also been given a new lease of life in 1938, converted to a 'Tevan' as figure 206, but this time for the conveyance of chocolates from Messrs. Frys of Bristol. The new Diagram was V.31, and the paintwork was white and red again. Dimensions were: 19'8" X 8'1", wheelbase 10', Tare 8T.8c. It was originally on Lot 429 of 1904 as X.2.

One of the meat vans which carried on in its original function was number 47967, and this picture shows the wagon in 1941, straight out of the paint shop after a major overhaul. Note the wartime livery. Originally built in 1889 to Lot 490, this means a useful life of at least 52 years! The dimensions on the wagon were 19'8" X 8'1", wheelbase 10', Tare 8T.4c.

Figure 208

Figure 209

130

An unusual cattle wagon of steel construction like the 'iron mink' with wooden doors. This vehicle was obviously an experiment, as it was part of a series of cattle wagons built under Lot 433 of 1888 and was the only one in this form. The photograph is dated July 1888, so is of the wagon as built. Note the grease axleboxes of the period. This wagon did not survive to be allocated a Diagram number. The painting was grey with white letters and roof.

Figure 210

An interesting picture of 1912 showing a line of cattle wagons of various designs and conditions, and which proves that at this date this type of vehicle had the lettering on the ends as well as the sides. For the record the numbers decipherable in the original photograph are as follows: left to right—number 68416, Diagram W.5; number 38666, Diagram W.1; number 38528, Diagram W.1; number 38102, Diagram W.3; number 13820, Diagram W.5; number 38266, Diagram W.1; number 38726, Diagram W.5; number 38353, Diagram W.1. (Figure 210)

Number 26001 is one of Lot 758 built in 1914 to Diagram W.8, code name 'Mex B', and the picture date is October 1916. There are several differences in the design from those in the top picture. Note that end bracing is now all angle irons, and the lettering on the ends has changed, number and size being painted in the centre panel, rather than on one side. The small red 'V' on the solebar indicates 'vacuum braked'. (Figure 211)

131

Figure 211

Figure 212

132

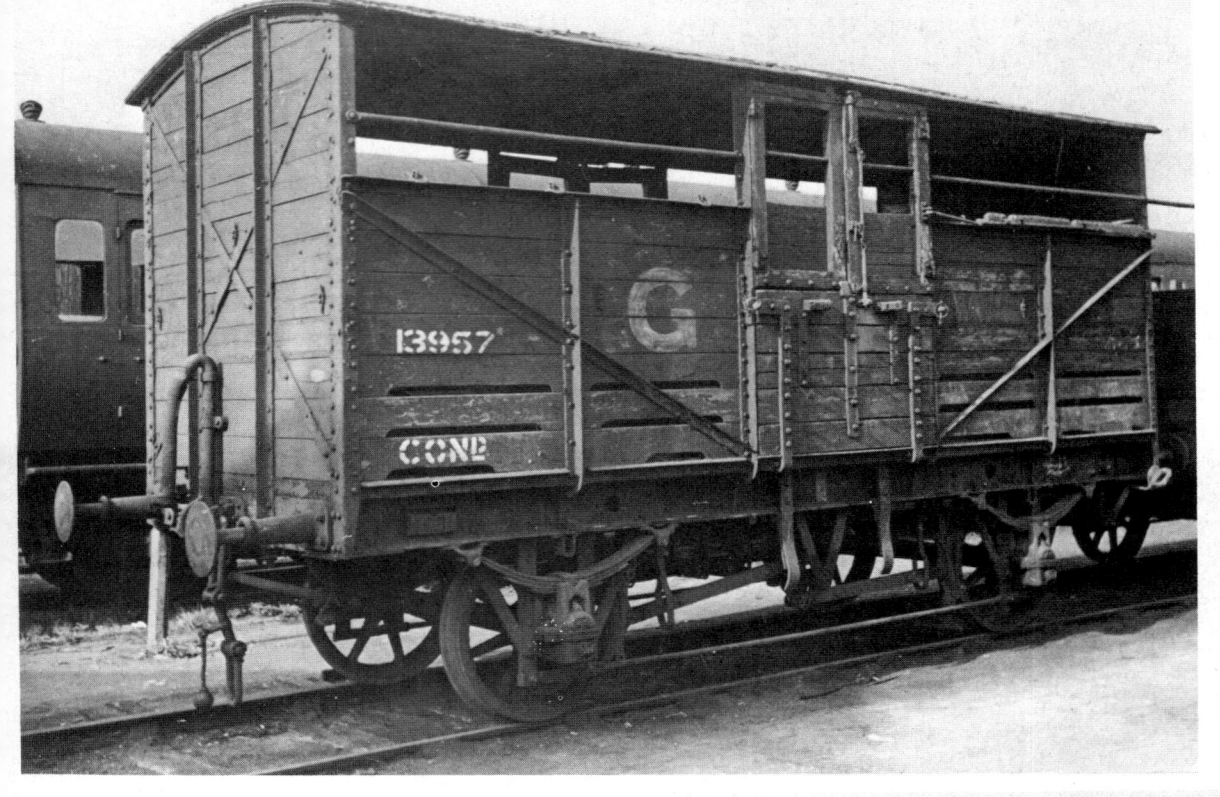

Two more 'Mex' in the cattle dock at Torquay in 1932, illustrating the end lettering still existing at that date. The flat roofed type is number 38833, and the arched roof number 103168. (Figure 213)

Figure 213

Figure 214

'Mex B' number 13957 at the end of its days in 1949 at Old Oak Common. Originally of Diagram W.5, its long life of half a century is showing badly, and the 'COND' inscription, meaning condemned, signifies the end of the road for this cattle wagon.

An official picture, dated 1922, showing the inside of a cattle wagon. The liberal use of lime-wash is very apparent; all such wagons after use had to be scrubbed out clean, and then daubed all over internally with the cleanser. It is possible to see that even the end walls up to the roof have been so treated!

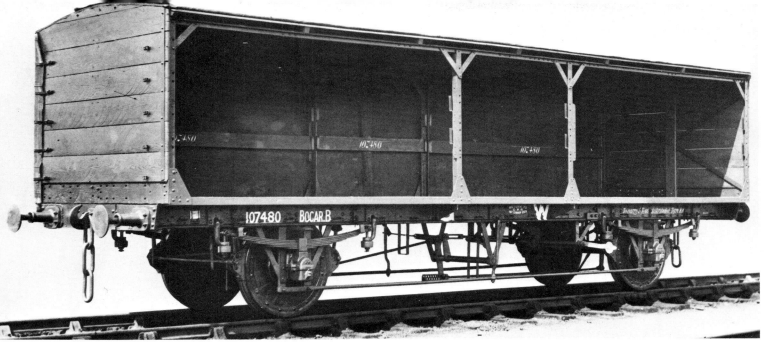

Figure 215

'Bocar B' was a four-wheeled version of the stock constructed, or perhaps it would be truer to state re-constructed, for the carriage of motor-car bodies from factories like the Pressed Steel Company Oxford for transporting to other factories for completion of the car building. Number 107480 is an example of the Diagram G.36, Lot 1156, of 1936 design, and with side sheets removed one can see the simple interior. Capacity loading was only 5 tons, Tare 8T.8c. (Figure 215). Originally the underframe was that of a four wheeled coach.

Figure 216

This figure shows a similar vehicle, as rebuilt yet again in 1944 and branded 'To work between Paddington Swindon and Clifton Bridge only'. Notice that side sheets have been fixed and double side doors have been fitted. Painting on these vehicles was black all over, with white lettering. (Figure 216)

Figure 217

134

Designed expressly for the carriage of rails, and originally given the code name 'Beaver D', number 48901 was a one only wagon. Built in 1890 to Lot 533, the Diagram allotted was J.3. It was 33' in length, with bogies of 5' wheelbase set at 23' centres; the load was 30 tons and the Tare weight 11T.12c. Note that only one bogie is fitted with a hand brake. The date of the photograph is given as 1910, but I would have thought it earlier. (Figure 217)

This similar vehicle is another 'one-off' job, being a 'Gane' of 1899, built to Lot 258, Diagram J.1. The photograph here is dated 1898, so this would picture the wagon at the shops when new. The plate on the side reads 'CONSTRUCTION DEPARTMENT'. The loading capacity was 40 tons with a Tare weight of 17T.7c. Dimensions were 45' in length, with 6' bogies set at 34' centres. Note that the bogie suspension side plates have been extended upwards to cover the sole-bar, and brakes are now on both bogies. (Figure 218)

Figure 218

Figure 219

Also a 'loner', number 41910, an armour plate or heavy roll wagon, was known in the code book as 'Totem A'. It was very solidly constructed to carry 45 tons, later increased to 50 tons. Dimensions were 22'1" over headstocks, 4'6" from rail head to wagon bed; bogies 6' wheelbase at 12' centres. The photograph is dated 1899, which was the building year to Lot 218, Diagram B.2. The two pictures show excellent detail, and would be useful for a good model. The plate with the small print reads 'When loaded, speed not to exceed 25 miles per hour or run more than 25 miles without stopping. As a rule they should be run in stopping trains. To be formed in train next to rear brake van.' (Figures 219 & 220)

Figure 220

During the First World War, the Great Western Railway sold, hired, and converted, many of its vehicles to the War Department for use in France and Belgium. One of these conversions is illustrated here, number 84603 of Lot 810, Diagram J.14, which was one of the 'Macaw B's, has been specially strengthened in the underframe for the conveyance of Army tanks. The raised wooden baulks on the ends were necessary for loading over the buffers at a loading dock, short timbers being placed in position over the buffing gear. There is no trace of this vehicle returning to the Great Western Railway. (Figure 221)

Figure 221

A similar conversion as figure 221, but this time with wagon number 84572 (5320 being a military numeral). The photograph is dated 1917. Built originally on Lot 810 as a 'Macaw B', number 84572 was given Diagram J.19 when converted. It was returned to stock at cessation of hostilities and re-converted to 'Macaw E', Diagram J.23. Note the Continental type drawgear. The paintwork was olive green, khaki.

Figure 222

Number 84105 was built in 1912 under Lot 685 to Diagram J.4. The picture, taken in 1917, shows the conversion to carry coastal motor vessels, hence the shaped chocks at ends and centre. The centre chock was adjustable up and down by means of a hand wheel under the chassis. The dimensions were 45' overall length, with 5'6" bogies at 35'6" centres.

Figure 223

This 'Macaw B', built in 1913 to Lot 743, Diagram J.14, was later converted for the carriage of 6" guns and timbers, as can be seen in this 1914 photograph. Loading over the end, the ramps can be seen on the left-hand side. Diagram J.17, number 84249, was eventually restored to the Great Western Railway and rebuilt as 'Macaw E'. (Figure 224)

Figure 224

Number 39226 was also converted to carry tanks, and the end detail is shown clearly here. Note that new rail head jacks have been fitted to take the weight whilst end loading. Also notice that Continental drawgear has been fitted. (Figure 225)

Figure 225

137

Figure 226

One of the later 'Macaws', the official photograph of number 107361 is of Lot 1189, built in 1937 to Diagram J.25. It was 35' long with 5'6" bogies at 25'6" centres; the load capacity of this 'Macaw H' was 20 tons, and the Tare weight 14T.15c. Painting was all over dark grey, with white letters and a red centre line on the solebar. (Figure 226)

An unusual 'Macaw' which only existed as such for six years. 'Macaw Z' was, in fact, built as a 'Bocar A' on an old coach underframe in 1934, on Lot 1155 as Diagram G.33. It was rebuilt as seen in 1940, to work as a rail wagon Diagram J.27, and then reconverted back to a 'Bocar A' in 1946. Evidence of the coach beginnings can be deduced from the Dean 6'4" bogies. (Figure 227)

Figure 227

An early picture of a 'Pollen A'. Built in 1888 to Lot 418, they started life as a twin, to carry 20 tons each. In 1890 two match trucks were added as inners, to make a four coupled unit. They were rebuilt again in 1906 as a twin unit to Diagram A.2. (Figure 228)

Figure 229

These two vehicles, 32994-5, were originally the inner twins of a four coupled set of boiler wagons, made in 1885 to Lot 331 and to Diagram A.3. In 1910 they were made into the double vehicle unit seen in the illustration, to Diagram A.7. The load was 12 tons each carriage; Tare 5T.8c. each. (Figure 229)

'Pollen C', numbers 48983-4, were a twin set of girder or boiler trucks, built in 1905 to Lot 515 as Diagram A.4. The load capacity was 20 tons each. Dimensions were 19' 2½'' over headstocks, with 9' wheelbase. (Figure 230)

139

Figure 230

This twin set was originally built in 1902 on Lot 379. They became Diagram A.1. after 1910, and in 1914 were fitted with swivelling carriages for the conveyance of naval guns. Each wagon had a capacity of 30 tons, and length over headstocks was 24'5"; wheelbase was 6' X 6' and Tare weight 11T.16c. The code name given to this set was 'Pollen B'. (Figure 231)

Figure 231

This was the largest of the Pollens, coded 'Pollen E'; it consisted of four wagons close-coupled together, and as shown is also arranged for the carrying of very large naval guns. (This wagon loaded with guns can be seen on page 143). Built in 1909 on Lot 608, the Diagram allotted was A.6. Each vehicle could accept 30 tons, but the limit with naval guns was 100 tons. The photograph is dated 1909. (Figure 232)

Figure 232

Numbers 32993 and 32996 were first constructed in 1885 as a four-coupled set to Lot 331, Diagram A.3. They were rebuilt in 1906 when bolsters were replaced by turntables for boilers, and were rebuilt again in 1910/11 as twin sets to Diagram A.7. The photograph was taken in 1916 and shows these two in this form. Loading was only 12 tons each vehicle, Tare weight 6T.1c. (Figure 233).

Figure 234 shows the Pollens in use at Chepstow in 1941, carrying three petrol storage tanks. Numbers 32991-2 were built in 1888 as twins, rebuilt in 1890 as four-coupled, and rebuilt again in 1906 as twins. Lots 418 and 528, Diagram A.5. Numbers 48981-2 were built in 1902 to Lot 379, Diagram A.1.

Figure 234

Figure 233

Figure 235

Pollens as girder wagons. This photograph, taken at Reading, shows 48903-4 supporting a huge girder on the turntables. The wagons were built in 1905 to Diagram A.4. (Figure 235)

This photograph, dated 1913, shows two more arched girders destined for overbridge work at Paddington. The leading wagons are numbers 48979-80, built in 1902 to diagram A.1. Each wagon had a capacity of 30 tons. (Figure 236)

Figure 236

Figure 237

over the River Thames at Kennington, and which in fact are still there! Notice the upright timbers, to give extra lateral support, not part of the bridge, but only for the journey by rail. The wagons are 48903-4, built in 1905 to Diagram A.4. Load 20 tons each, Tare 7T.9c. Note the number and letters on the buffer beam. (Figure 237)

'Pollen E' carrying the naval gun for which the cradles were made; picture dated 1909. Later on, in 1930, this four-coupled set was divided into two sets of twin wagons. The numbers were 84998-99 and 84997-85000. Drawings of the vehicles in this form can be found on page 63 of *A Pictorial Record of Great Western Wagons*.

Figure 238

Numbers 56 and 59 are a pair of close-coupled 'Mites'. Built in 1888 to Lot 416, the Diagram J.9 was allotted to these wagons. They were 15′ in length with a 7′ wheelbase and designed for the primary job of timber carriage. The load was 10 tons each, and the Tare of the two was 9T.16c. (Figure 239)

Figure 239

Figure 240

Another pair of 'Mites', photographed in 1910. Numbers 48265 and 48266 were constructed in 1896 to Lot 36, also to Diagram J.9 (although early ones of the series were running in 1894). Dimensions were 18′ length with 7′ wheelbase. Capacity 10 tons each, code name 'Mite B'. (Figure 240)

Figure 241

This picture shows two 'Mites' converted in the 1914-18 war, for the conveyance of coastal motor boats. By the look of the springs, the timbers and chocks alone form a good load, even before the extra weight of the craft is added! (Figure 241)

Figure 242

'Gadfly' was the code name for this long four-wheeled vehicle, rebuilt for the carriage of aircraft! Originally this wagon was a 'Beaver C' with six wheels (see page 102 of *A Pictorial Record of Great Western Wagons*), and in 1916 the centre pair of wheels was removed and the Diagram H.5 was allotted. Later still it was used for dock traffic. A drawing of this wagon can be found in *A Pictorial Record of Great Western Wagons*, on page 129.

Another rare wagon was the 'Mayfly', shown in this picture of 1920. Six vehicles were made in all, numbers 94670/1/2/3/4/5/.The Diagram was G.23 and the purpose of the design was for the conveying of electric transformers. Dimensions were 18' over headstocks, 7'1" in clear in well, with a wheelbase of 11'6". Tare 5T.16c (official drawing in *A Pictorial Record of Great Western Wagons*, page 129).

Figure 243

Figure 244

146

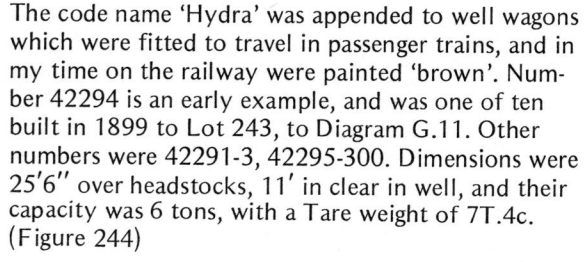

The code name 'Hydra' was appended to well wagons which were fitted to travel in passenger trains, and in my time on the railway were painted 'brown'. Number 42294 is an early example, and was one of ten built in 1899 to Lot 243, to Diagram G.11. Other numbers were 42291-3, 42295-300. Dimensions were 25'6" over headstocks, 11' in clear in well, and their capacity was 6 tons, with a Tare weight of 7T.4c. (Figure 244)

This is a later 'Hydra D', built in 1917 in a series numbered 42185-95. The Diagram was G.22, end sizes were 28'6" over headstocks, 15' in well, 8'9" width, 22'6" wheelbase. To carry 15 tons; Tare weight 8T.10c.

Three pictures of 'Hydras' taken by Mike Longridge in 1950. Number 42296 in figure 246 was seen at Tyseley yard loaded with a road construction machine, and number 42297 in figure 247 shows the wagon empty at Old Oak Common. Both vehicles were to Diagram G.11 and Lot 243, and were built in 1899. 'Hydra D', seen in figure 248, was also at Old Oak Common sidings when photographed. This is number 42194 and again is of Diagram G.22. Note that this wagon was fitted with a steam pipe for working on passenger trains. The dimensions on the wagon are 32'6" X 8'8", wheelbase 22'6", Lot 745 of 1917.

Figure 247

Figure 248

Figure 249

Number 42142 was one of the 'Loriot D' well wagons built in 1908 to Diagram G.18. This vehicle had a capacity of 15 tons with a Tare weight of 8T.7c, and a 21' wheelbase. Pictured at Old Oak Common in 1950. (Figure 249)

'Loriot L' also had a loading capacity of 15 tons, and was constructed in 1929 to a series of seven, numbering 42231, 42269-74, to Diagram G.13. Number 42272 is seen at Swindon yard in 1952, still carrying Great Western Railway plates. (Figure 250)

Figure 250

This shows number 42273 straight out of the shops in 1929 and gives good detail of the painting of these wagons, which was grey all over with white lettering.

Figure 251

Figure 252

This picture of an early 'Loriot' has the bonus of
vintage stock in the background! 'Loriot A',
number 42001, was first built in 1889, under Lot 491
to Diagram G.2, along with forty similar wagons,
numbers 42002-40, and later transposed in 1910 to
'Loriot B'. The load was 12 tons, and Tare weight
5T.18c. Note the trussing under the solebars.

Figure 253

Next in line of numbering and building was the
'Loriot B' design of 1891 to Diagram G.1, Lot 562.
Ten were built, with numbers 42041-50, which in
1916 became 'Loriot D'. The load capacity was 15
tons and the Tare weight was 7T.4c. (Figure 253)

Figure 254

Jumping ahead fifty years, 'Loriot W' was constructed in 1944 to Lot 1441. Only two were made,
numbers 100701 and 100703. The Diagram was
G.41. They were designed for the Engineering Dept. at
Hayes creosoting yard, and long crossing timbers
often used these wagons as transport. The dimensions
were 31'6" over headstocks, 20' clear in well. They
were of 20 tons capacity, the Tare was 13T.11c.

149

Figure 255

Also to Diagram C.10 were numbers 33988-9, 33991-34000, and 41911-41914 of Lot 198, built in 1899. Eventually eight were passed to the traffic dept. and renumbered 41979-86, code name 'Crocodile'. This picture shows 33988 as new in 1899. Note the swivelling coupling hook. (Figure 255)

You may well ask 'what is it?' In fact it is a vehicle made up of various bits, to act as an inspection trolley for use in the Severn Tunnel. The wagon is a boiler trolley dating back to approximately 1870. Number 92 was possibly made on the Loco dept. Lots. There were three similar, 93, 106, and 107 to Diagram C.10. The dimensions were 34′ over headstocks, 24′6″ in well × 5′3″, with 28′ wheelbase. The load consists of an old Birkenhead Railway saloon with four standard gas tanks, plus flares for lighting.

Figure 256

Figure 257

Roll wagons, vehicles made specifically for the transport of heavy steel rolls or ingots *en route* to rolling mills. Number 32289 is one of such made by the Great Western Railway in 1933 to Diagram B.8.

Figure 258

Number 32114 is another design of roll wagon, but this time made from an old tender chassis of the Rhymney Railway, with the centre wheels removed. The load capacity was 15 tons, and Tare 9T.1c.

A similar wagon, and from the same ancestry, number 32127 was a one-only wagon, which originally had six wheels and ran behind a locomotive on the Rhymney Railway. All three wagons were photographed at Swindon in 1949.

Figure 259

Figure 260

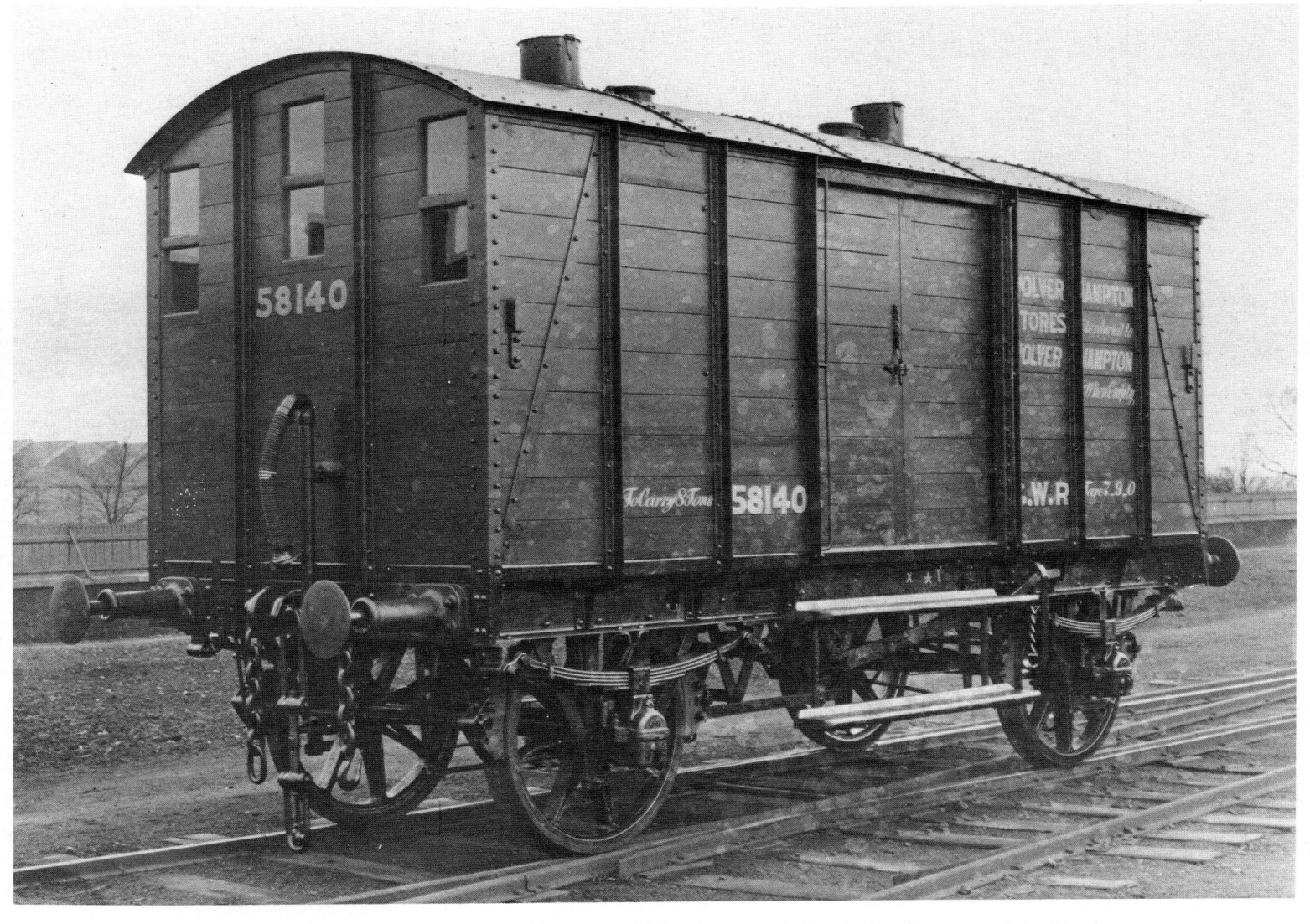

An early stores van of approximately 1887 period. Wolverhampton being the headquarters of the Northern division, locomotive, and Civil Engineer's departments, it was general practice to send small stores to out-lying stations in vans of the type shown here (very much akin to the mobile shop of today). The vehicle, although numbered in the wagon list, could also travel on passenger trains, as witness the vacuum brake and screw shackles. Painting would probably be brown with yellow lettering. Note the oil pot lamps in the roof and the end windows to let in light.

Figure 261

Number 14992 is one of the 24′ tool vans used by the Signal dept., for use when they were performing work along the line of route. Built under Lot 812 of 1915, the Diagram was C.C.7, and there were three such vehicles 14990/2. Wheelbase was 17′ and they were fitted with a small jib inside the doors. Painting was black and white. (Figure 261).

Figure 262

Another type of tool van, this time for the Loco. Dept. for use on breakdown or derailment jobs. It was built in 1913 on Lot 718 to Diagram C.C.8, and fitted with end doors. It was 28′6″ in length with an 18′ wheelbase, and was painted brown with a white roof. Note the skylights. (Figure 262)

153

Figure 263

154

Although this tool van is numbered DW 80987, I rather think that it is one of the same series as figure 261 because all the dimensions and general design are identical. This could probably be the renumbering received under British Rail, and perhaps the previous number was either 14990 or 14991. The photograph was taken in 1950 at Tyseley.

A new use for crane match trucks? Number 86, seen here at Old Oak Common in 1949, is transporting three steel hoppers used for concreting. (Figure 264)

Figure 264

Figure 265

A mobile steam plant? A transportable tar sprayer? Fish and chip parlour? No, this vehicle is none of these, being in fact a travelling compressor! An upright boiler for raising steam, to supply an engine, which drove a pump to compress air, for the Engineering Department to use with pneumatic tools! Note the take-off points around the right-hand side and end of the plant. The coiled hose is for use as a water lifter to supply the boiler via a tank from any wayside source. The photograph is dated 1903 and the wagon number is 14938. Painted black all over, with white letters.

Figure 266

156

This special van was one of five, built in 1942 to Lot 1397, for the C.M.E.'s department. The numbers were 184-8 and dimensions were 24'0½" length × 7'8½", with a 16' wheelbase. The vans contained a complete diesel pump installation, and were for use during the war at the South Wales Docks. This end of the vehicle shows the water inlet and outlet, and also the exhaust gas pipe.

Figure 267

This picture illustrates the opposite side to that in figure 266. Here can be seen the gangway, which could be coupled up to a mess van or staff coach. These vans often ran with a specially-built oil fuel tank. Tare weight of the vans was 32T.5c—quite a heavy loading. Note that as well as double swing doors, two more upward opening doors are fitted on this side, whereas in figure 266 three upward openings are the sum total on the reverse side.

Figure 268

158

Starting now with a section of the permanent way rolling-stock, what more apt than to illustrate the most humble of all wagons, and yet the one that is always there at the laying down of any railway! Number 58 is one of the side-tipping dumper wagons of the construction gangs. Built to Lot 119 in 1896, the diagram given was P.8. As can be seen, this wagon would only tip one way, and was balanced so that this operation could be achieved easily by several workmen. All ironwork was painted black with white lettering; all timber was left unpainted.

Figure 269

A very early loco coal wagon, inserted here to show a comparison with the contemporaneous all-steel Permanent Way ballast wagon. Number 9408 is one of Lot 417, built in 1887/8 to Diagram N.6, of 10 ton capacity, Tare weight 5T. The photograph is dated 1888. Note the early horse box over the left buffer.

Number 14168 was built in the same period as the loco coal wagon, number 9408, to Lot 446 and allotted Diagram P.5. In length it was 16', with a 9' wheelbase; capacity was 8 tons, and Tare weight 4T.18c. Note the flaps over the springs and axle-boxes to prevent ballast dust causing abrasions. Both these vehicles were painted black with white letters.

Figure 270

Figure 271

160

Figure 272

One of the early bottom-doored hopper wagons of the Great Western Railway, number 40957 was constructed in 1893 to Lot 20 and given Diagram P.7. Twenty were made to this order, the numbers being 40951-60, 40971-80. Notice again the ballast flap over the running gear. (Figure 271)

This photograph of number 60005 was taken in 1937 and illustrates clearly the development of the hopper wagon over 45 years. The Diagram is still P.7 as above, and all that has happened to the design is that raised sides have been fitted on top to give greater capacity. Oil boxes have taken the place of the grease, and heavier springs allowed 20 tons to be carried instead of 8 tons. In addition, vacuum cylinder and either-side brakes have been added, and so brought the hopper up to date. But, note how the pattern of bodywork is exactly the same as the 1894 version. Lot number 30. (Figure 272)

Another in the Lot 20 series of 1893, number 40971 is shown here as it illustrates the fact that these ballast hoppers had the bottom door gear on one side only, with the hand-brake on the opposite side; it was only the introduction of the either-side brake which enabled brake handles to be fitted on both sides. It is also interesting to note the different lettering style on this example compared with figure 261. Load 12 tons, Tare 5T.12c. (Figure 273)

Figure 274

Figure 273

An early, large, 20-ton hopper of the Diagram P.6 design. The picture is dated 1903 and shows the fitting of the early style of quick-release patent brake. Note the steps at one end and hand rails, and that the ballast flap over springs is still retained.

Figure 275

162

A three-quarter view of the same wagon as that in figure 274, to show more detail of the end and the running gear. According to the available records, there was only one made to Lot 371 of 1902, so this seems to suggest an experimental prototype.

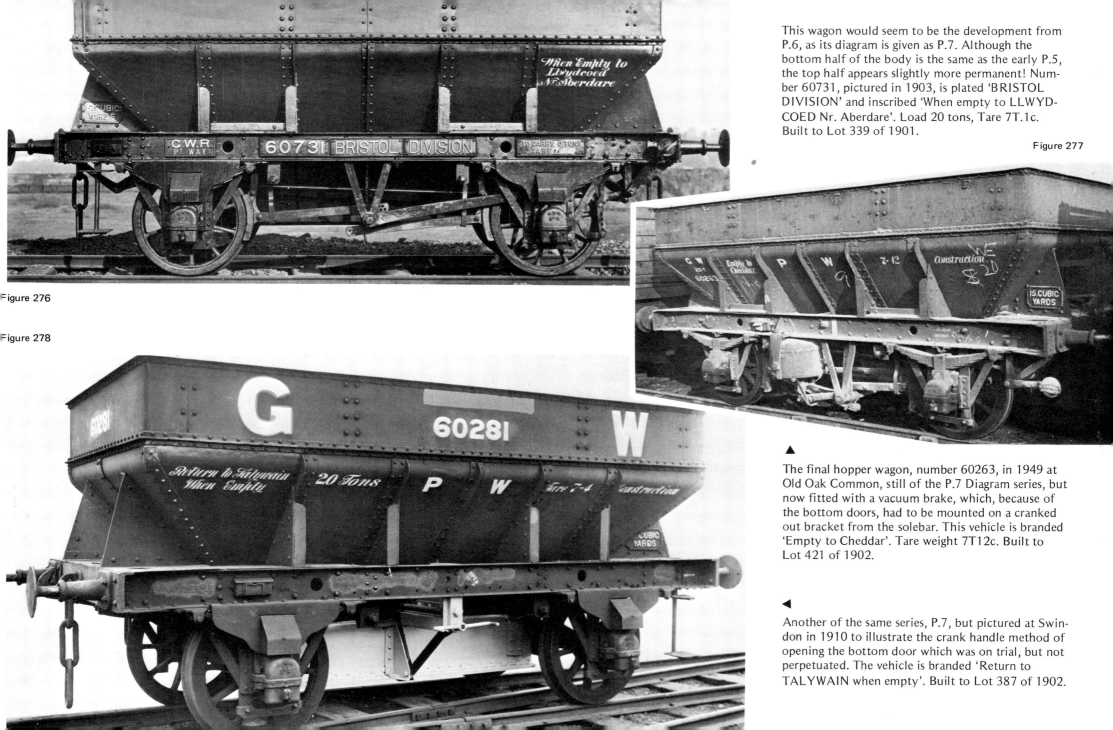

This wagon would seem to be the development from P.6, as its diagram is given as P.7. Although the bottom half of the body is the same as the early P.5, the top half appears slightly more permanent! Number 60731, pictured in 1903, is plated 'BRISTOL DIVISION' and inscribed 'When empty to LLWYD-COED Nr. Aberdare'. Load 20 tons, Tare 7T.1c. Built to Lot 339 of 1901.

Figure 277

Figure 276

Figure 278

The final hopper wagon, number 60263, in 1949 at Old Oak Common, still of the P.7 Diagram series, but now fitted with a vacuum brake, which, because of the bottom doors, had to be mounted on a cranked out bracket from the solebar. This vehicle is branded 'Empty to Cheddar'. Tare weight 7T12c. Built to Lot 421 of 1902.

Another of the same series, P.7, but pictured at Swindon in 1910 to illustrate the crank handle method of opening the bottom door which was on trial, but not perpetuated. The vehicle is branded 'Return to TALYWAIN when empty'. Built to Lot 387 of 1902.

An early all-steel Permanent Way Department ballast or spoil wagon, pictured at Swindon in 1902. Capacity 14 tons, Tare weight 7T.3c. It was fitted with three drop doors on each side and had covers over the running gear. (Figure 279)

Figure 280

Figure 279

A special wagon for the carriage of crossing timbers during construction or the re-laying of trackwork. Note the absence of any doors and the high strengthened ends, to take the end thrust of the long baulks. Tare weight 5T.18c. (Figure 280)

Figure 281

Figure 282

Three small ballast or spoil wagons are seen on this page, of all-steel construction and two are of Diagram P.15. No. 80240, at the top right, was photographed in 1939, and that at bottom right in 1949. Number 14555 is similar but earlier, being to Diagram 14, and has no lip on the top edge of the sides. This official picture is dated 1926. All three wagons were of 10-ton capacity.

Figure 283

Figure 284

166

Slightly larger than the previous three wagons, number 30789 was capable of carrying 14 tons and was of more modern design, being fitted with disc wheels and even had the facility of a step at one end. It is seen at Old Oak Common in 1949. The Tare weight was 7T17c. Built in 1944 to Diagram P.21, to Lot 1434.

Number 14071 was a design to Diagram P.12, according to the register at Swindon, having a length of 21′ and a wheelbase of 12′. Its capacity was 20 tons and the Tare weight was 8T.5c. The date of the picture is 1920. Note that this wagon is fitted with vacuum brakes and 'Instanter' couplings. Built to Lot 555 of 1907. (Figure 285)

Figure 285

Figure 286

Another early ballast wagon similar to that in figure 285. This series was built in 1904 under Lot 465 to Diagram P.12. It was of 14 tons capacity, and the Tare weight was 7T.4c. Branded 'Wolverhampton Division' when photographed at Swindon in 1922.

Number 14105 is one more of the Diagram P.12 design. Built in 1907 on Lot 655, the dimensions were 21' in length, 12' wheelbase, with a 20 ton capacity and a Tare weight of 8T.6c. Branded 'Return to COALBROOK DALE WESTERN VALLEYS'.

167

Figure 287

Figure 288

One final example of the low-sided ballast or spoil wagon. Number 14351, a small 10-tonner belonging to the London Division, was originally constructed in 1913 under Lot 712, to Diagram P.14. Its length was 16′ and the wheelbase 9′. Tare weight only, 5T.12c. The date of the picture was 1927. (Figure 288)

Figure 289

Another later example of a long four-wheeled wagon made for the carriage of long crossing timbers, number 14451 was to Lot 794 of 1914, of the Diagram J.12 design. The wheelbase was 20′, and other dimensions were 30′6″ length by 7′6″ width. This was photographed in October of 1914, so it would be brand new, even in front of the Lot date. There were three drop doors on each side, and also the two ends could be lowered onto the buffer shanks. Owing to the very long wheelbase, the wagon was branded to the effect 'This vehicle must not be close-coupled on any curve less than 3 chains radius. Return empty to Hayes Creosoting Yard'. 14 tons capacity, 8T.18c. Tare. (Figure 289)

I like this picture of the old Aveling & Porter and its attendant water cart with the sprinkler at the rear—very nostalgic, as I once owned a steam roller! However, the wagon upon which the roller sits, number 41000, was built in 1897, to Diagram F.2. It was 40' over headstocks with 4'6" bogies at 30'6" centres, load 25 tons. Three others were made—numbers 40998-9 on Lot 197 of 1897, and number 40996 of Lot 353 in 1901. (Figure 290)

The 'Loriot R' shown was made for a similar purpose to Diagram F.1 in 1904, to Lot 470. A fellow, number 40995, was built earlier in 1903 to Lot 412, and number 40993 to Diagram F.3 on Lot 723 in 1913. Number 40992 was rebuilt to the condition shown in the photograph in 1913 on Lot 753 to Diagram F.4, and finally renumbered in 1928. Dimensions were: 40' length, 15' in well, 5'6" bogies, capacity 25 tons, Tare 16T.17c. (Figure 291)

Figure 291

A special well-wagon, made for the purpose of transporting chaired sleepers, number 40476 is one of the early design without ends, and is illustrated complete with a full load. The picture is dated 1896 and it can be seen that the capacity of the wagon was 16 tons with a Tare weight of 8T.16c. (Figure 292)

Figure 292

Figure 294

Figure 293

Two identical sleeper wagons, but photographed in 1949 at Old Oak Common. Numbers 40422 and 40437 both have steel ends fitted, as it was found that sleepers could work out endways whilst *en route*. The load capacity was up to 18 tons and they both bear a plate stating 'TO CARRY 160 CHAIRED SLEEPERS'. These wagons were amongst the few to retain the custom of numbers and letters being painted on the ends. Painting was always black with white letters.

The Signal Department, based at Reading, had quite a fleet of special wagons for the conveying of signal posts and gear from the signal works to site. Number 14977, built to Lot number 132, to Diagram T.3, was one of these. With rigid sides of 15″ height and a very long wheelbase, they were distinctive vehicles. This example has a crank handle brake, and a small trussing on the chassis. The load was 14 tons and Tare 6T.12c. The photograph is dated 1898. (Figure 295)

Very much like 14977 is this two-plank wagon of the Permanent Way Dept. Photographed in 1933 when adapted for use as a weed-killing unit, number 40141 had a capacity of 10 tons and a Tare of 5T.12c.

Figure 295

Figure 296

Rail wagons for the use of the Engineering Dept. were known as 'Ganes', and in this official picture we see number 100698, one of the series made in 1938 on Lot 1290 to Diagram J.26, 'Gane A'. Numbers ran concurrently from 100689-700, and the dimensions were 62' length, bogies 5'6" at 51'6" centres. The load was 40 tons and Tare weight 22T.3c. Painting was black with white letters, and a red band along the steel side plate. (Figure 297).

Figure 297

Re-laying track used to be extremely hard work when sleepers and rails had to be man-handled off and on to the rail wagons, so it was a great help when, in the thirties, a system was devised to load old rails by means of engine-power. The 'Macaw' was moved close to the ends of the rails to be loaded and the brakes secured hard on; then by means of a long cable and chain, which was fastened at one end to the rail and at the other to the engine's coupling hook, the engine moved off and so drew the rail up and on to the rail wagon. This picture of 1932 illustrates the operation well.

These two pictures show 'Gane A' wagons with two different loads. In the top illustration prefabricated track is seen, ready for off-loading at site, which in this case was at Magor, facing the Severn Tunnel, in 1948. The two wagons shown are numbers 30734 and 100534. In the lower photograph is number 30737 carrying a small load of rails at Banbury in 1952. This was built to Lot 1378 of 1940, Diagram J.29.

Figure 299

Figure 300

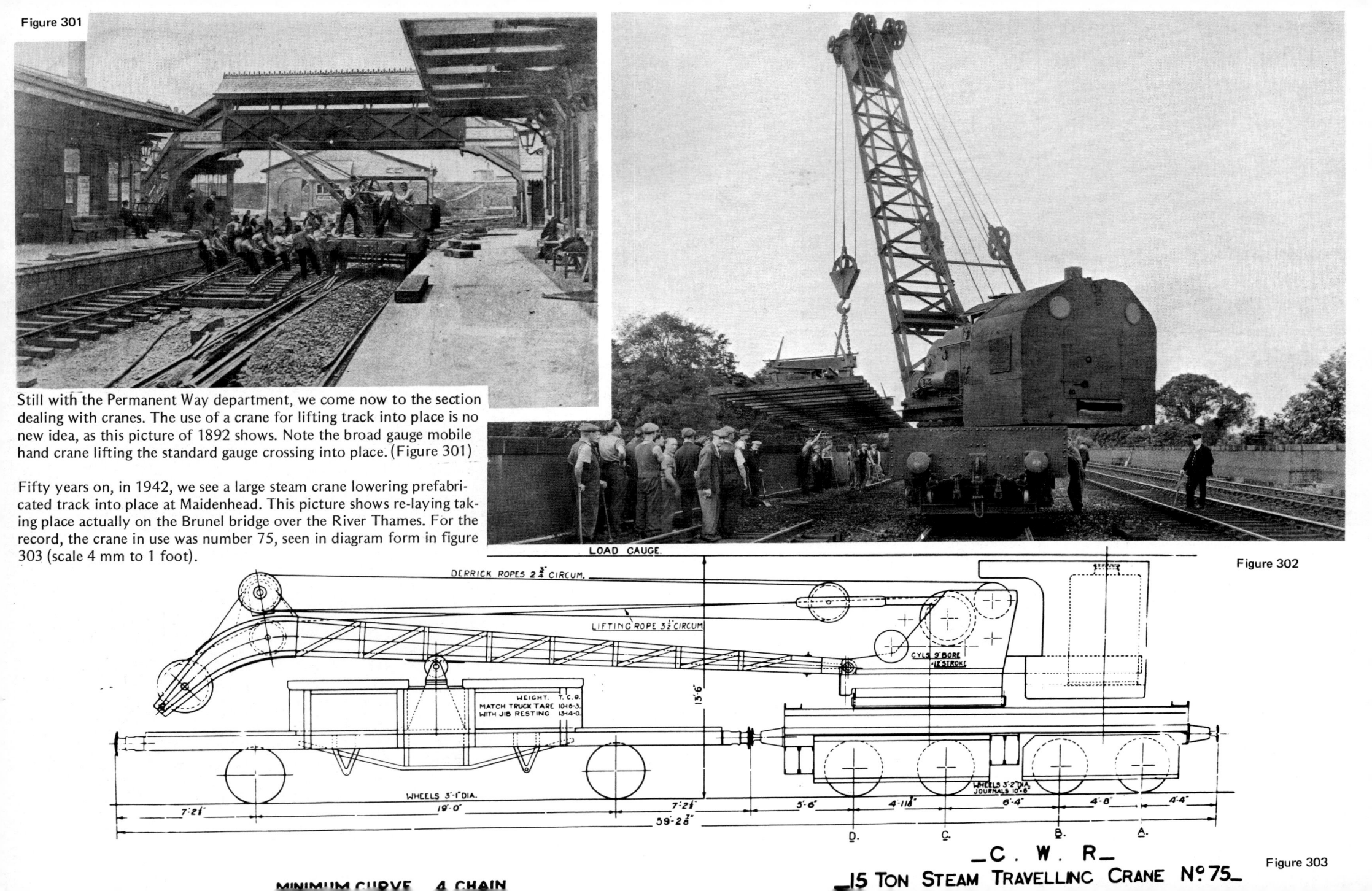

Figure 301

Still with the Permanent Way department, we come now to the section dealing with cranes. The use of a crane for lifting track into place is no new idea, as this picture of 1892 shows. Note the broad gauge mobile hand crane lifting the standard gauge crossing into place. (Figure 301)

Fifty years on, in 1942, we see a large steam crane lowering prefabricated track into place at Maidenhead. This picture shows re-laying taking place actually on the Brunel bridge over the River Thames. For the record, the crane in use was number 75, seen in diagram form in figure 303 (scale 4 mm to 1 foot).

Figure 302

LOAD GAUGE.

DERRICK ROPES 2¾ CIRCUM.

LIFTING ROPE 3½ CIRCUM

CYLS 9 BORE 12 STROKE

15'6"

WEIGHT.   T. C. Q.
MATCH TRUCK TARE 10·16·3.
WITH JIB RESTING 15·14·0.

WHEELS 3'·1" DIA.

WHEELS 3'·2" DIA.
JOURNALS 10·8"

7'·2¼"   19'·0"   7'·2¼"   5'·6"   4'·11⅝"   6'·4"   4'·8"   4'·4"

59'·2⅝"

D.   C.   B.   A.

_ C. W. R _
15 TON STEAM TRAVELLING CRANE No 75

Figure 303

MINIMUM CURVE 4 CHAIN

Another delightful photograph from the Civil Engineers' archives. Crane number 67 is shown at work in the centre road at Shrewsbury. The work in progress is the lifting of the roof trusses of the station. Note the timber-framed brake van in the station.

Figure 305

A fixed yard crane in use. The self-conscious staff are engaged in loading pipes at Pangbourne station. Note the large platform which swings around with the crane. The leading wagon is Match truck number 32173, and the vehicle being loaded is a 'Macaw'. Notice the station building and cattle dock on the left of the picture. The photograph is dated 1942.

Steam crane number 7 of broad gauge days, shown in the timber yard at Swindon in 1890. These were the spacious days as one can see by that lovely glazed cabin, and how about that tall, copper-capped chimney and the locomotive whistle! The gallant crew look like members of a Gilbert and Sullivan opera. Note the coupling rods and dumb buffers. Load capacity 6 tons.

Figure 306

Figure 308

A contrast in mobile crane capacity! Number 1, in the upper photograph, was built in 1901 by Cowans Sheldon & Co. Ltd. of Carlisle. For breakdown and general use, the maximum capacity was 15 tons. When the large 36-ton cranes were purchased in 1910, the number was changed to number 8, and it was stationed at Newton Abbot. The Tare was 55T.15c.

The small hand crane, shown at Swindon in 1896, would be of very small loading; there is no decipherable branding, but I would consider 1½ tons would take it to the limit! A similar crane has been preserved on the Dart Valley line. (Figure 308)

This illustrates the Cowans steam crane number 1 with the jib lowered and ready for travelling with its attendant match truck. Maximum radius for this crane was 20′ with a 5 ton loading when free and 26′ with a 10 ton loading if jacked. It was withdrawn in 1960. The match truck was to Diagram L.4. Tare 8T.13c. (Figure 309)

Figure 310

Number 75 is another 15-ton steam crane, but this one was manufactured by J. Booth & Bros. of Radley, Leeds, in 1926. Having a longer jib, the radius capability was naturally greater than the Cowans in figure 248. Maximum radius was 30′ load 6 tons propped, or 3 tons free. This machine was allocated to the Docks Engineer, Cardiff. The match truck used for this unit was to Diagram L.19, Tare 10T.1c.

Figure 311

Figure 312

Another photograph of crane number 75, showing the jib erected at a 25' radius, ready for work, match truck moved away. (Figure 311)

A different style of mechanism and jib is shown in number 12. Of Wilson manufacture, its capacity was 12 tons at the short radius seen in this photograph. The chassis was of the 0—8—0 classification, and cylinders were mounted upright. Maximum radius and load, proposed, was 30' and 6 tons respectively. It was stationed at Swindon. The paintwork when new in 1909 as photographed, was grey and white details, but later black all over.

Figure 314

In direct contrast is this massive 45-ton steam breakdown crane of 1945, also at Swindon, lifting a test load wagon in the crane yard. Made by Ransomes & Rapier, its number was 151, and the wheel formation with bogies was 4—8—4. Twelve similar were built for the four Railway Companies, of which the Great Western Railway had four. The scheme was to enable these cranes to work anywhere on any Company's system. (Figure 313)

With jib at maximum radius, unpropped, the load was down to 3 tons only, and this 1909 picture shows this position clearly. Note the diagonal bracing on the inside of the jib, and the half-picture of number 111 'The Great Bear' moving onto the turntable at Swindon Shops. (Figure 314)

A complete breakdown unit, which was stationed at Old Oak Common for many years. Crane number 5 was of Cowans & Sheldon construction of 1903, but the photograph is dated 1907. The capacity of the crane is 20 tons and maximum radius free was 20', increasing to 26' propped. The match truck is Diagram L.4, and the large bogie mess-cum-tool van is branded 'Loco Carriage & Wagon Dept Old Oak Common'. The colour scheme for these vans was milk chocolate brown body with black underframe, white roof, and yellow ochre lettering, with the ends signal red. The roof board was painted black with white lettering. (Figure 315)

Figure 315

A final shot of number 12, the Wilson 12-ton steam crane, in the travelling condition with attendant match truck to Diagram L.12. The chimney, which is shown erected, would of course be dismantled and lie flat on the cab roof whilst *en route*. (Figure 316)

Figure 316

Figure 317

Figure 318

In 1910 the Great Western Railway Company acquired two very large steam cranes, both of 36 tons capacity. One of these machines was built by Stothart and Pitt of Bath. In this official photograph it is seen in the travelling condition. The jib was firstly of the lattice type, changed by 1917 into plate girder. The wheel arrangement was 0—6—4, with a bogie match truck under the jib which was built to Diagram L.11, and a long four-wheeled wagon to carry the outrigger girders was provided to Diagram L.10. This crane was numbered 1 and the open runner 1A. This meant that the original number 1 on page 179 had to be re-numbered! After trials at Swindon, this unit went to Old Oak Common, replacing number 5, and was stationed there until 1941 when it was transferred to Bristol; it ended its days at Worcester.

This is the second 36-ton crane, purchased at the same time as number 1, and it naturally was given the numeral '2'. See next page for details.

For the benefit of modellers, this diagram of number 1 gives many of the relevant dimensions, scale 4 mm to 1 foot.

Figure 319

Figure 320

All steam cranes supplied to the Great Western Railway were required to undertake a test lift of 25% above their working load, before being accepted by the Company. In this historic picture we see this test being applied. Cranes numbers 1 and 2 are jointly lifting 'The Great Bear' which scaled no less than 97 tons without the tender! This picture then proved visually that the two cranes were capable of 48½ tons each. Crane number 2 was built by Ransomes & Rapier in 1908 and was always stationed at Swindon. In the lower illustration we see the complete breakdown unit, comprising match truck Diagram L.10, the crane itself (right-hand side), bogie match truck to Diagram L.11, and the long bogie mess-and-tool van, number 132. Roof boards confirm 'Loco, Carriage and Wagon Dept., Swindon Factory'. These bogie vans were 62' in length, divided internally into four compartments: one for messing, another for the officers in charge, a third for tools and equipment, and a fourth for the guard, fitted with a hand brake. 40-ton and 20-ton jacks were provided, usually of the traversing type with a swivelling base, plus all tools, chains, flares, gauges, Red Cross equipment, and fire extinguishers, etc. One of these vans still exists at Oxford Loco shed. Both numbers 1 and 2 had their wheels, axles, axle boxes, buffers, and drawgear supplied by the Great Western Railway.

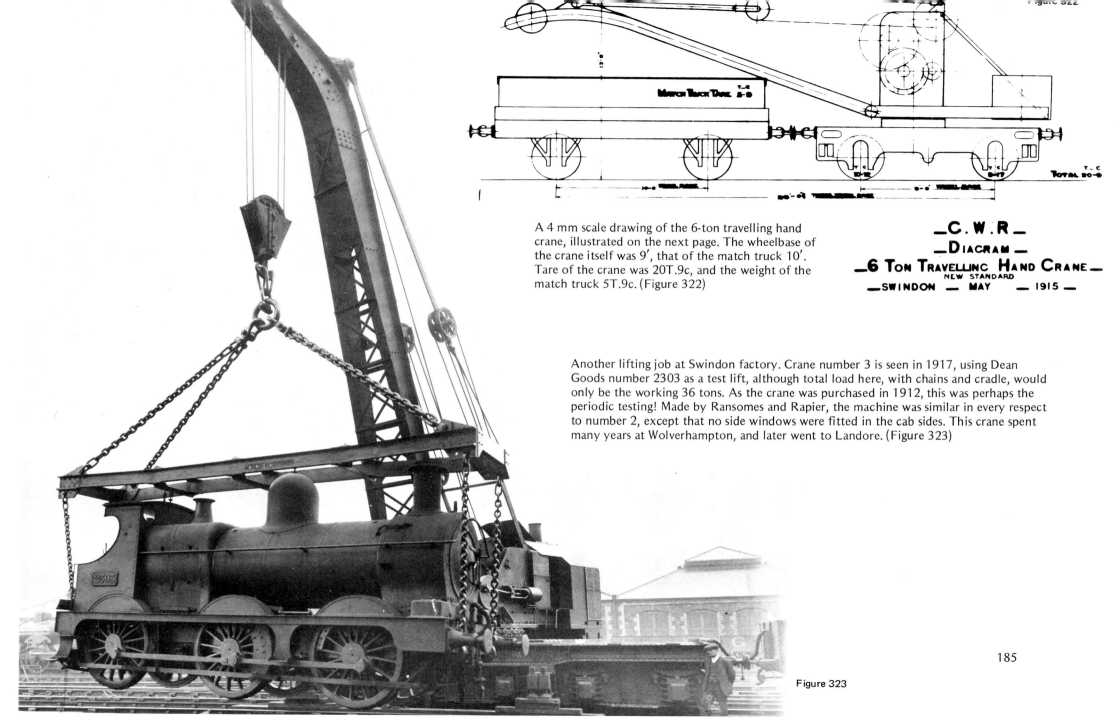

A 4 mm scale drawing of the 6-ton travelling hand crane, illustrated on the next page. The wheelbase of the crane itself was 9′, that of the match truck 10′. Tare of the crane was 20T.9c, and the weight of the match truck 5T.9c. (Figure 322)

_C.W.R_
DIAGRAM
6 TON TRAVELLING HAND CRANE
NEW STANDARD
_SWINDON — MAY — 1915 —

Another lifting job at Swindon factory. Crane number 3 is seen in 1917, using Dean Goods number 2303 as a test lift, although total load here, with chains and cradle, would only be the working 36 tons. As the crane was purchased in 1912, this was perhaps the periodic testing! Made by Ransomes and Rapier, the machine was similar in every respect to number 2, except that no side windows were fitted in the cab sides. This crane spent many years at Wolverhampton, and later went to Landore. (Figure 323)

185

Figure 323

Six wheels support this travelling hand crane, which had a capacity of 12 tons. The platform attached to the jib head was for the examination of tunnel roofs, as can be seen in 'Track Topics', the Great Western publication, on page 170. Note that the balance weight was on rollers, and could be moved along a track to give more or less the weight as required. This crane was number 207, with a Tare weight of 32T.17c, which in 1936 was allocated to the Loco Dept. at Swindon.

▼

Figure 325

Figure 324

▲

The small 6-ton hand crane depicted here was made by Willetts Junr. of Cradleigh Heath for the Great Western Railway in 1915, and would seem to be as per the drawing on the previous page. The fixed balance weight and hinged wooden platforms can be seen. Notice the stone carvings of broad gauge engines on the wall of the drawing office behind. Date of the photograph—1928. (Figure 324)

Figure 326

Every crane, be it hand or steam operated, when travelling along the line of route with jib down, naturally had to be coupled to a special vehicle which would not only act as a check wagon for the long overhanging jib, but also carried the weight of this girder whilst in the down position. As curves were taken, so the jib moved sideways on the match truck, so provision had to be made to allow the jib carriage to slide across the wagon. In this picture we see number 211 (which was not only the number of the wagon but also that of the crane it attended), made in 1914 to Diagram L.3.(Figure 326)

Of the same general pattern, but shorter, is number 8, shown in three-quarter view, to give a good sighting of the jib carriage and its slide. This shorter match truck was to Diagram L.15. Both pictures are dated 1914.(Figure 327)

Figure 327

Even longer is match truck number 26, built to Diagram L.16 in 1914. Of very long wheelbase, this vehicle has some light trussing under the centre line, and the usual four compartments, with drop down doors, which contained ropes, chains, and slings, etc., as well as shackles and various timber packing.

Figure 328

A slightly later version of the long wheelbased match truck, number 57 was to Diagram L.19 and dated 1919. Given angle iron bracing, and parallel buffers, this wagon is fitted with 'Instanter' couplings instead of the usual screw shackles. (Figure 329)

Figure 329

After the glamorous huge breakdown cranes, we finish with this lowly steam crane, used for coaling locomotives by bucket when the coaling stage was out of action for some reason. I've seen this being done at both Swindon and Oxford. Details of the machine are undecipherable, but dimly the number 102 can be seen on the side.(Figure 330)

This photograph of 1942 shows three of the wagons which were converted from flats in 1938 to form vehicles for the carriage of aircraft 3-bladed propellers. Code named 'Aero', there were four batches: 1938, numbers 137692-6; 1938, 137672-91; 1940, 141669-718; 1941, 139197-296. In this photograph, left to right, are number 137692 empty, number 137694 loaded, and number 137696 also empty. When their use as propeller carriers came to an end they were reconstructed as open wagons in 1950.

▼

Figure 330

Figure 331

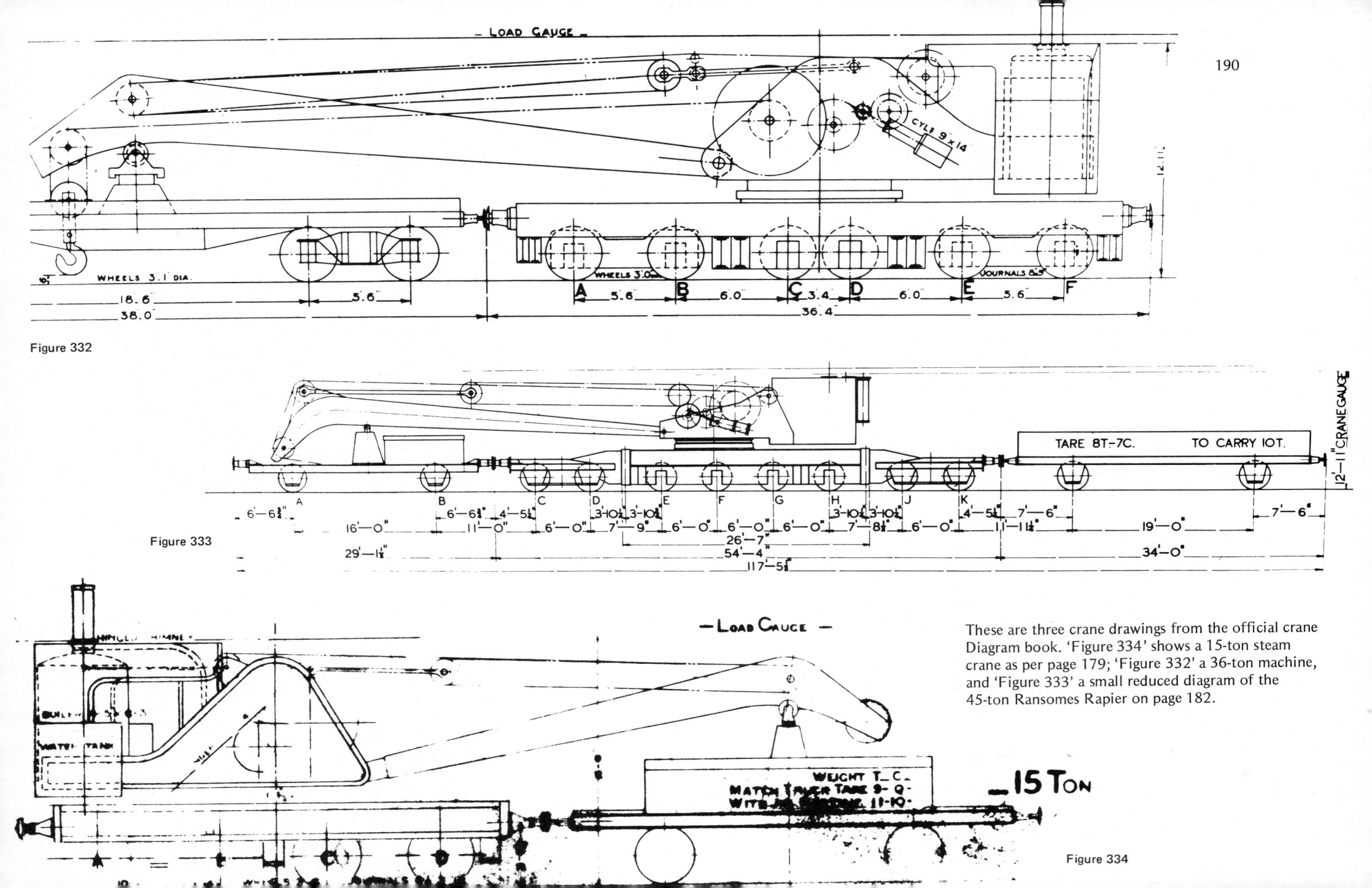

— LOAD GAUGE —

CYLS 9 x 14

WHEELS 3.1 DIA

WHEELS 3.0

JOURNALS 8.9

| A | | B | | C | D | | E | | F |

6"

18.6

5.6

5.6

6.0

3.4

6.0

5.6

38.0

36.4

12.11

Figure 332

12'—11" CRANE GAUGE

TARE 8T—7C.   TO CARRY 10T.

| A | | B | | C | D | E | F | G | H | | J | | K |

6'—6¼"

6'—6¼" 4'—5½"

3'—10½" 3'—10½"

3'—10½" 3'—10½"

4'—5½" 7'—6"

7'—6"

16'—0"

11'—0"

6'—0"

7'—9"

6'—0"

6'—0"

6'—0"

7'—8½"

6'—0"

11'—11½"

19'—0"

26'—7"

54'—4"

34'—0"

29'—1¼"

117'—5½"

Figure 333

— LOAD GAUGE —

SINGLE CHIMNEY

BUILT

WATER TANK

WEIGHT T_C_
MATCH TRUCK TARE 9-Q-
WITH JIB PACKING 11-10-

_15 TON

WHEELS

JOURNALS

These are three crane drawings from the official crane
Diagram book. 'Figure 334' shows a 15-ton steam
crane as per page 179; 'Figure 332' a 36-ton machine,
and 'Figure 333' a small reduced diagram of the
45-ton Ransomes Rapier on page 182.

Figure 334

Figure 335

Figure 336

A final page of details. Top left picture shows a close-up of small-headed self-contained buffer. Top right the early small wagon buffer and coupling hook, without provision for removing the chain links

◄ A close-up detail of the 'Churchward' ratchet brake handle and lever.

Brake gear, and the inscription on chain locker of 'Conflat' wagon number 39368. The small star was to indicate the position of the vacuum brake release cord, and the letters 'XP' showed that this vehicle could run on passenger trains under special conditions.

▼

Figure 338

Figure 337

INDEX